Amazing Shark

Michael Stavarič ✦ *Michèle Ganser*

AMAZING SHARK

GUARDIAN OF THE SEAS

Pushkin Children's

CHAPTER
01

OUR JOURNEY NEVER ENDS

Infinite spaces. Infinite knowledge. Infinite ways to tell all about it.

Do you remember the first time you saw the sea? That seemingly endless expanse, glittering and sparkling; nothing but glistening water stretching as far as the horizon? And above it, our beautiful Sun, with a bright-blue postcard sky and a few cheeky seagulls? I remember it clearly: for me, it was the Mediterranean, on a beach near Podgora in what is now Croatia! It's a moment you will never forget, no matter how old you get.

Looking at the sea makes you realize how incredibly lucky we are to live on a "Blue Planet". Our Earth is often called that. And it does look like a blue planet, especially when seen from space. There is blue, sparkling precious water everywhere, which is anything but typical in the vastness of our universe.

Liquid water only exists in the so-called "habitable zone"—this is what scientists call the distance a planet (our Earth, for example) must be from its sun for water to remain permanently liquid. If our Earth were too far from the Sun (outside this habitable zone), all water would freeze immediately. And if our Earth were too close to the Sun, then all water would evaporate.

The habitable zone is no big mystery. It simply means a place where we and all other living things can live.

But perhaps there are other life forms in the vastness of the cosmos that require entirely different "habitable zones"? For example, maybe there are life forms that don't need water to live and are not affected by heat, cold, radiation, etc. That would also make the concept of the habitable zone" completely pointless! And the idea is not completely far-fetched. I was reading something about "extremophiles" on our planet recently, and it made me think about this whole issue in a new way. Let me explain this very quickly: extremophiles are organisms that can live under the most extreme environmental conditions—for example, in boiling water (!), in corrosive acids (!), in salt solutions, under high pressure, etc.

My favourite extremophile (a word borrowed from the Greek, by the way, meaning "lover of extreme conditions") is definitely the tardigrade. This little creature can easily withstand strong radiation and exist in a vacuum (airless space). Consequently, scientists have speculated whether it could survive permanently in space (e.g. on the Moon)! Tardigrades live in the ocean, of course, as well as almost everywhere on Earth! I love tardigrades! Such fascinating little critters!

In *Amazing Octopus* and *Amazing Jellyfish*, I already told you a lot about how everything is connected: the cosmos with our planet, the sea with our origins. We talked about evolution and all kinds of scientific knowledge and disciplines, and we encountered lots of land and water animals… So what can we expect in this book?

Well, I don't really know myself yet. It will involve sharks, of course, but I promise we'll find out the rest together.

You'd better get yourself a drink and some biscuits. Does anyone need to go to the loo?

Go on, then. Quickly now!

Ready? Ready! Then let's go on an expedition—to the incredible world of sharks!

Now That's What I Call "Long in the Tooth"

Some time ago (at Christmas) I received a lovely present: a tooth. Now, don't go thinking that I grew a new tooth or something. I'm way too old for that. And I didn't get a new false tooth at the dentist either. Don't get me wrong—false teeth are cool. If they are well made, they are crafted from ceramic (like beautiful teacups) or even pure gold (wow!). No, I was given the tooth of a famous, long-extinct, enormous animal… and it's been on my bedside table ever since!

Sometimes, I pick it up and marvel at it, because it is almost as big as the palm of my hand. That would probably make it as big as your whole hand! Maybe I'll show you this tooth if you come to one of my events with your parents. I'll definitely be taking it along. It is—drum roll!—the tooth of a magnificent megalodon.

Those of you who already know what a megalodon is—and I'm sure that includes all my favourite bright minds—will learn more about this extinct species a little later. But for everyone else: megalodons were the largest sharks that have ever lived on our planet, although we can only guess just how massive the biggest megalodon was, because no fossilized shark skeletons have ever been found. Unlike dinosaurs and other prehistoric animals (sabre-toothed tigers, for example—which also have cool teeth) prehistoric sharks (like modern ones) usually only left their teeth behind in the oceans.

You see, sharks are "cartilaginous fish", which means their "bones" are actually made of cartilage rather than bone, like your ears or the tip of your nose! For now, we just need to remember that cartilage is flexible and tough, but too soft to be preserved as fossils.

I can't list all the (more than 520!) known shark species here, so you'll have to search for your favourite sharks yourself, but scientists classify sharks into eight orders:

1. Ground sharks (more than 270 species), 2. Bullhead sharks (nine species), 3. Frilled & cow sharks (seven species), 4. Mackerel sharks (seventeen species), 5. Carpet sharks (approximately thirty-four species), 6. Saw sharks (nine species), 7. Dogfish sharks (more than 113 species) and 8. Angelsharks (eighteen species).

Some shark scientists list a ninth order of sharks, the Bramble sharks. They have thorns on their skin, like the plant they're named after. There are only two species in the entire order, and they are large and slow and live very deep in the ocean. Since they're so reclusive, let's also leave them be.

Finally, for the sake of completeness (because we're not in the business of doing things by halves here): the class of Cartilaginous fish also includes rays and ratfish. In other words: sharks, rays and ratfish are related to each other. There are around 630 known species of rays and around fifty-five species of ratfish (but none of them can cook a decent ratatouille).

Incidentally, sharks keep growing throughout their lives, so they are never really fully "grown up" like us—and some can get very old (more on that later).

There are, of course, other animals that grow all their lives: crocodiles, anacondas, lobsters, king crabs, elephants and kangaroos, for example. People often say that our noses and ears keep growing all our lives, but that is nonsense. However, a doctor once explained to me that as we get older, the tissue in

AMAZING SHARK 11

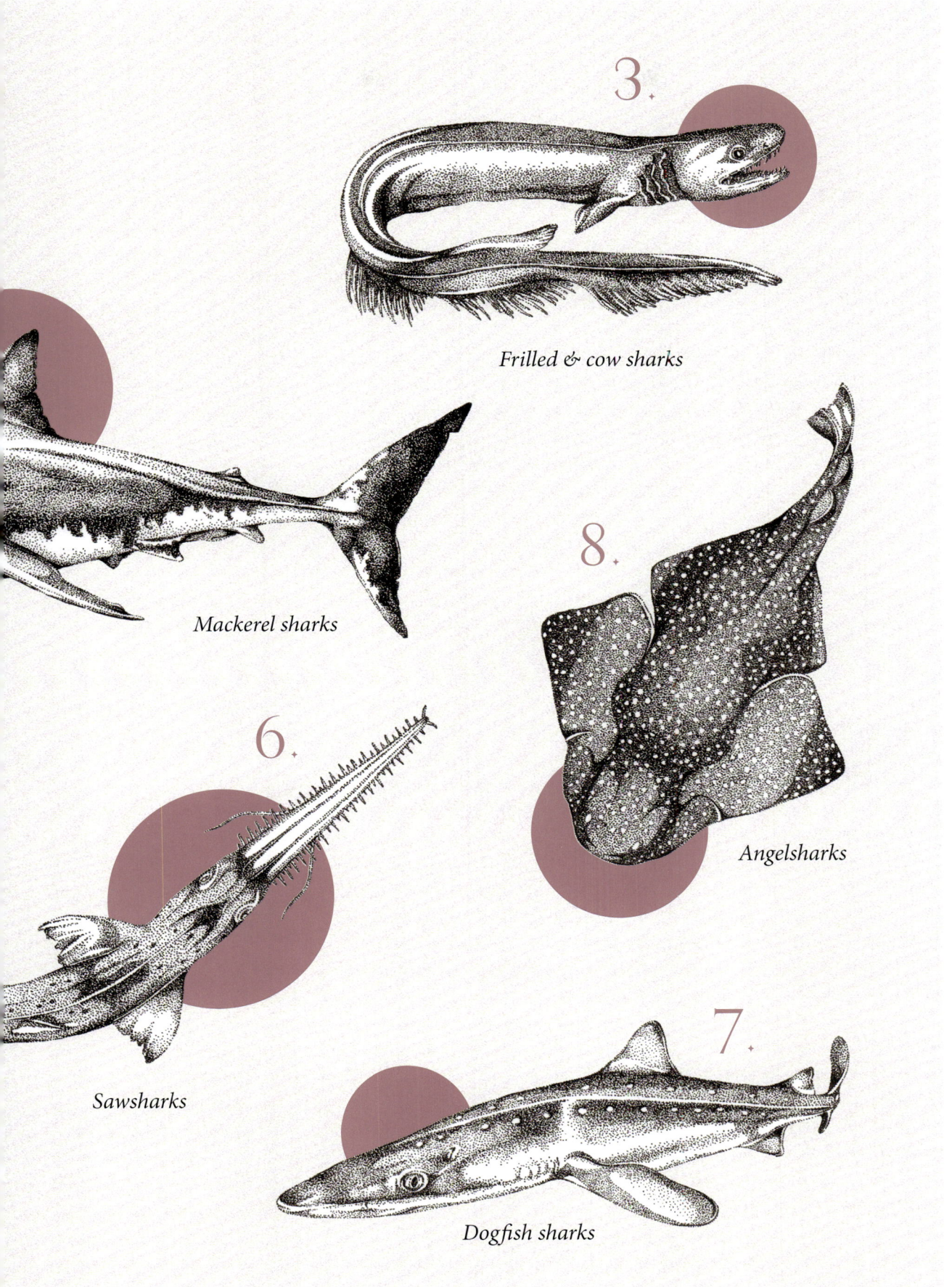

3.
Frilled & cow sharks

Mackerel sharks

8.
Angelsharks

6.
Sawsharks

7.
Dogfish sharks

Can you find all seven cartilaginous fish hiding here? Solution: p. 134

our noses and ears becomes flabbier, and gravity then stretches these parts of the body, allegedly by about one centimetre in fifty years. So, two centimetres every 100 years. That is not all that bad.

But let's hurry back to the megalodon's teeth, which are so tough that they have survived for millions of years. Human teeth are also the toughest parts of our bodies. And because each person's teeth are absolutely unique (like a fingerprint), a skilled dentist can use a photograph to match teeth (or a dental impression) to a specific person. So they can say: "Yes, indeed, these are the teeth of Michael Stavarič. Without a doubt. No chance of a mix-up." Oh, and before I forget: "Megalodon", like many scientific terms, is borrowed from the Greek and means "big tooth".

This would have made a good name for a Native American chieftain, don't you think? They had very similar (and I think great-sounding) names. Want some quick examples? Of course! How about Stumbling Bear (of the Kiowa Apache)? Or Leg in the Water (of the Cheyenne)? Or Bear Tooth (of the Crow)? Or Ten Bears (of the Comanche)? Or His Eyebrows Stick Out (of the Iroquois)? Or "Tecumseh", the "Blazing Comet" (Chief of the Shawnee)? Incidentally, the latter had an older sister, also a chief, because everyone listened to her. Her name was "Menewaulaakoosee Tecumapease", which translates as "flies over the water". And we'd better fly on now. There are still so many exciting things to discover…

Megalodon 101

Did you know that the great white shark is to blame for the megalodon's extinction? Scientists discovered in 2022 that both shark species were apex predators (meaning they were at the top of the food chain) at the same time—and that the great white shark eventually prevailed.

A normal-sized megalodon (measuring around fifteen metres long) had a huge dorsal fin that was 1.6 metres high and two metres long. Its weight would have been somewhere between 50—100 tonnes. (Just like us humans, some were slimmer and some a bit beefier than others.) Its total height was a good 4.5 metres (including the dorsal fin). Incredible, isn't it? And its life expectancy was around eighty to 100 years.

The power of a megalodon's bite is just as legendary—a 100-tonne specimen would have a bite ten times as strong as that of a great white shark and at least three times as strong as a T-Rex. Today's animals don't come close, although the great white shark still has the greatest bite force in the world today. It can bite with a force of around 1.8 tonnes. That's the weight of your average car. The alligator and crocodile are in second place—they can bite with a force of up to 1.6 tonnes. And then comes the hyena (one of my favourite animals)—it can bite with the force of almost a tonne. Oh, and adult humans can bite with a force of up to eighty kilograms. That's if they always brushed their teeth as children. And now let's all pick up one of those biscuits (which I hope you have ready) and put it in our mouth. Imagine it's a tough whalebone and take a bite. Welcome to the world of the megalodon! Or the great white shark. Cool, right? (*And try not to leave too many crumbs!*)

Just recently (January 2023), the news was full of pictures and stories of nine-year-old Molly, who discovered a thirteen-centimetre-long shark tooth on a stretch of coastline in the US state of Maryland. The family took it to a marine museum where they were told that the tooth was about 15 million years old and came from a megalodon roughly fifteen metres long. I mean, what a great find, right? Incidentally, the largest teeth ever found were seventeen centimetres long. Why don't you take a tape measure… wait, actually, I have a better idea. Michèle? Could you please draw us a seventeen-centimetre megalodon tooth here? Thank you!

One thing I wanted to tell you: when I'm having a bad day (and who doesn't have those), I pick up the megalodon tooth, run my fingers over it and imagine that this huge creature was never afraid of anything in its life. And you know what? It makes me feel better! It's like some of that "megalodon courage" has been transferred to me.

Let's always be brave, and remember: it's much easier to do that together than alone!

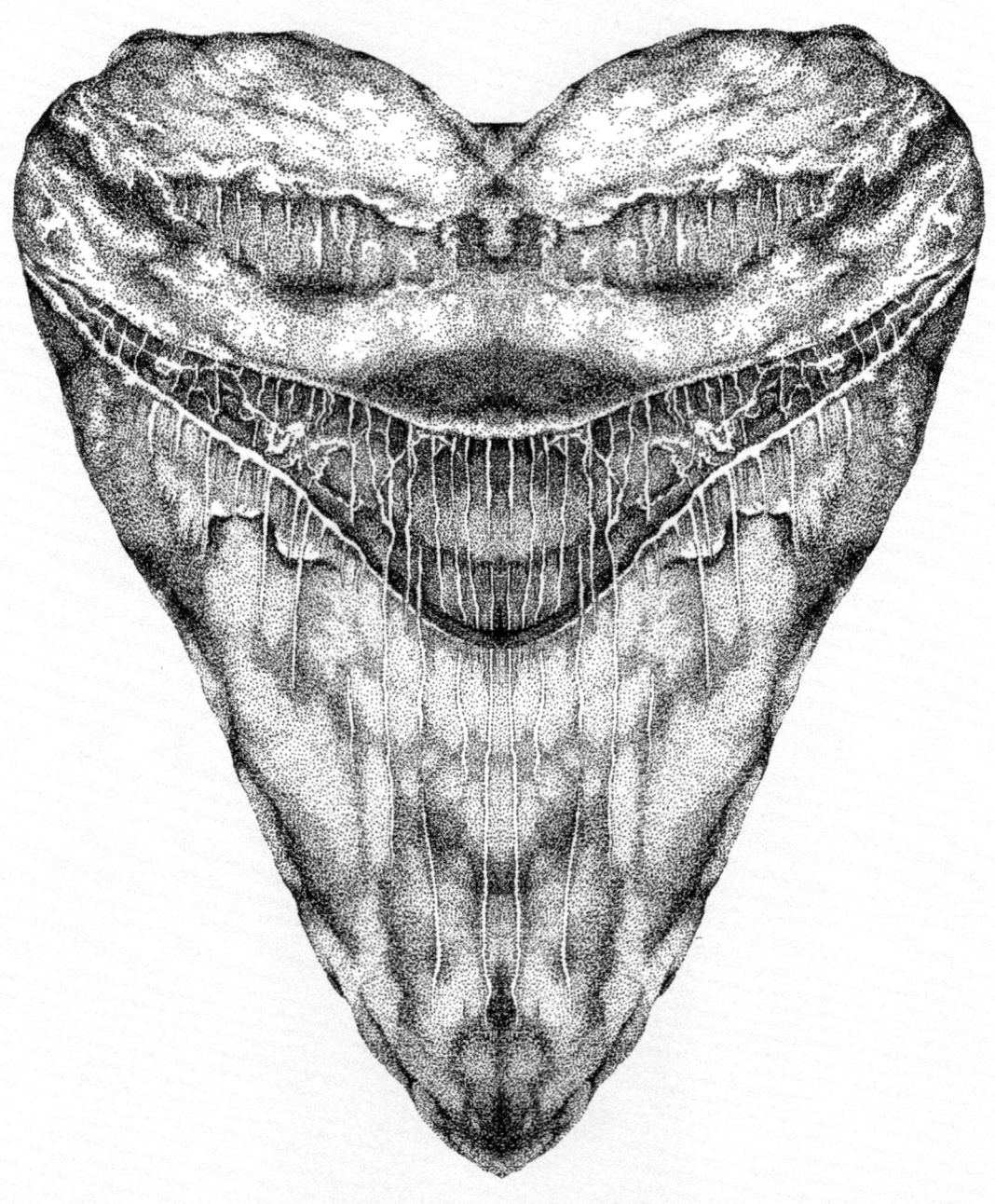

Megalodon tooth

Sayings with teeth crop up regularly in our language—can you tell me what they actually mean here? (Answers on p. 133)

1. A tooth for a tooth.
2. Getting long in the tooth.
3. By the skin of your teeth.
4. As bad as pulling teeth.
5. To lie through your teeth.
6. To fight tooth and nail.
7. To have a sweet tooth.

What Exactly Is "Revolver Dentition"?

The jaws of a shark (extinct or not) are absolutely amazing—they keep growing teeth throughout their lives. It's as if they have an escalator in their mouth that keeps pushing new teeth forward as the old ones wear out. In science, this is called "revolver dentition". I don't particularly like guns, so let's call it "escalator dentition" from now on. Besides, I like taking the escalator. Do you? Just imagine an escalator but with teeth instead of steps. That's how sharks' teeth work. And I bet you want to know how long it takes for a broken tooth to be completely replaced. It varies from shark species to shark species and can take anywhere from a week to several months. In total, a shark uses up to 30,000 teeth in its lifetime! Wow! I wish I could grow new teeth too. Then I would never have to go to the dentist again. And I'd never have to brush my teeth either.

Since we're on the subject of shark teeth: many people are terrified of getting bitten by sharks in the ocean. The so-called "tabloid press" (a term used to describe newspapers with a very over-the-top style) is not the only place where you read stories that suggest that sharks are constantly attacking people. This is utter nonsense! First of all, sharks are not interested in us humans as prey because the animals they naturally prey on are (and taste) completely different: whales, seals, fish, turtles, etc. And secondly, there are really very few unpleasant incidents with sharks, all of which are not shark attacks but shark accidents. If a shark happens to bite a human somewhere, then almost all the media worldwide report on it—and you get a completely false idea of how dangerous the animals are for us humans.

You must understand that sharks are curious (and quite clever) creatures and they don't have hands. So the only way they can examine anything they find in the ocean is with their mouths (and teeth). Sometimes sharks nibble on something really carefully to find out what it is—and their sharp teeth can cause serious injuries. Sometimes, a shark may also feel threatened by a human because they are swimming into their territory—basically, they want to get them out of their home quickly. It can also sometimes happen that a shark actually mistakes a human for one of its prey animals, such as a seal or a sea lion.

If you're out on the water on a surfboard wearing a dark wetsuit with your hands and feet outstretched, well, to a shark below, you will look a lot like a sea lion. The shark may attack, but it will usually quickly realize its mistake.

Unfortunately, by then, the accident may have already happened. I am positive that if sharks could talk, they would apologize for their mistakes.

Anyone in the world who takes sharks seriously (divers, fishermen, photographers, biologists, etc.) will tell you that the label "man-eater" is completely wrong for these animals. So maybe you should delete this term from your vocabulary!

Let me prove this with a few numbers: in 2022, fifty-seven shark accidents were recorded worldwide—five of which were unfortunately fatal. In the previous year, seventy-three shark accidents were recorded—with nine fatalities. In all other years, the figures look pretty much the same. We can compare this with other animals and statistics to put these accidents into context. But first things first: all the experts in the world absolutely agree that the probability of a person being involved in

22 FANCY A BONUS ROUND?

Can you find all of the seven species sharks like to prey on? Solution: p. 136

a shark accident is 1 in 11.5 million. So it's about as likely as winning the lottery jackpot.

I studied a statistic from 2016 (but other years are similar), according to which most human deaths caused by animals were caused by mosquitoes. 725,000, in fact. 50,000 deaths were caused by snakes, 25,000 by dogs, 10,000 by tsetse flies, 10,000 by assassin bugs (yes, that's what they're called), 10,000 by snails (poisonous ones), 1,000 by crocodiles, 100 by elephants, twenty by horses and so on.

I don't even want to tell you how many people worldwide die from cat bites every year. But of course, what everyone was talking about in 2016 were the ten shark accidents. Do you see how absurd that is? On average, twenty-four people die every year from being hit in the head by a champagne cork, toasters kill around 700 people a year, and lightning strikes kill around 2,000 people.

To humans, at least, sharks are the least dangerous creatures in the world. This is despite their impressive strength, their sharp teeth, and the fact that millions of people regularly swim in the oceans where millions, perhaps more than a billion, sharks live.

Don't get me wrong—sharks are very strong and dangerous animals, but the truth is that they coexist surprisingly

peacefully with us humans, especially when you consider that, like us, they also like to swim close to the beach. From now on, please help me change their bad reputation. The next time you hear an adult panicking about possible shark attacks, why don't you enlighten them with the help of statistics? Here's another fact: in the UK alone, at least 6,000 people die every year as a result of household accidents (i.e. falling off ladders, touching electrical wires, etc.).

Oh, by the way: according to American bite statistics, up to 2 million dog bites are registered every year, followed by around 400,000 cat bites. Human bites (i.e. where people bite other people!) are estimated to total at least 40,000 and maybe as much as 400,000 a year. It is safe to say that significantly more people die from dog, cat and human bites (infections!) than from shark accidents!

Please stop being afraid of sharks. This fear is absolutely unfounded. And promise me one thing: don't let your fears tell you what to do. Fear is not a good guide.

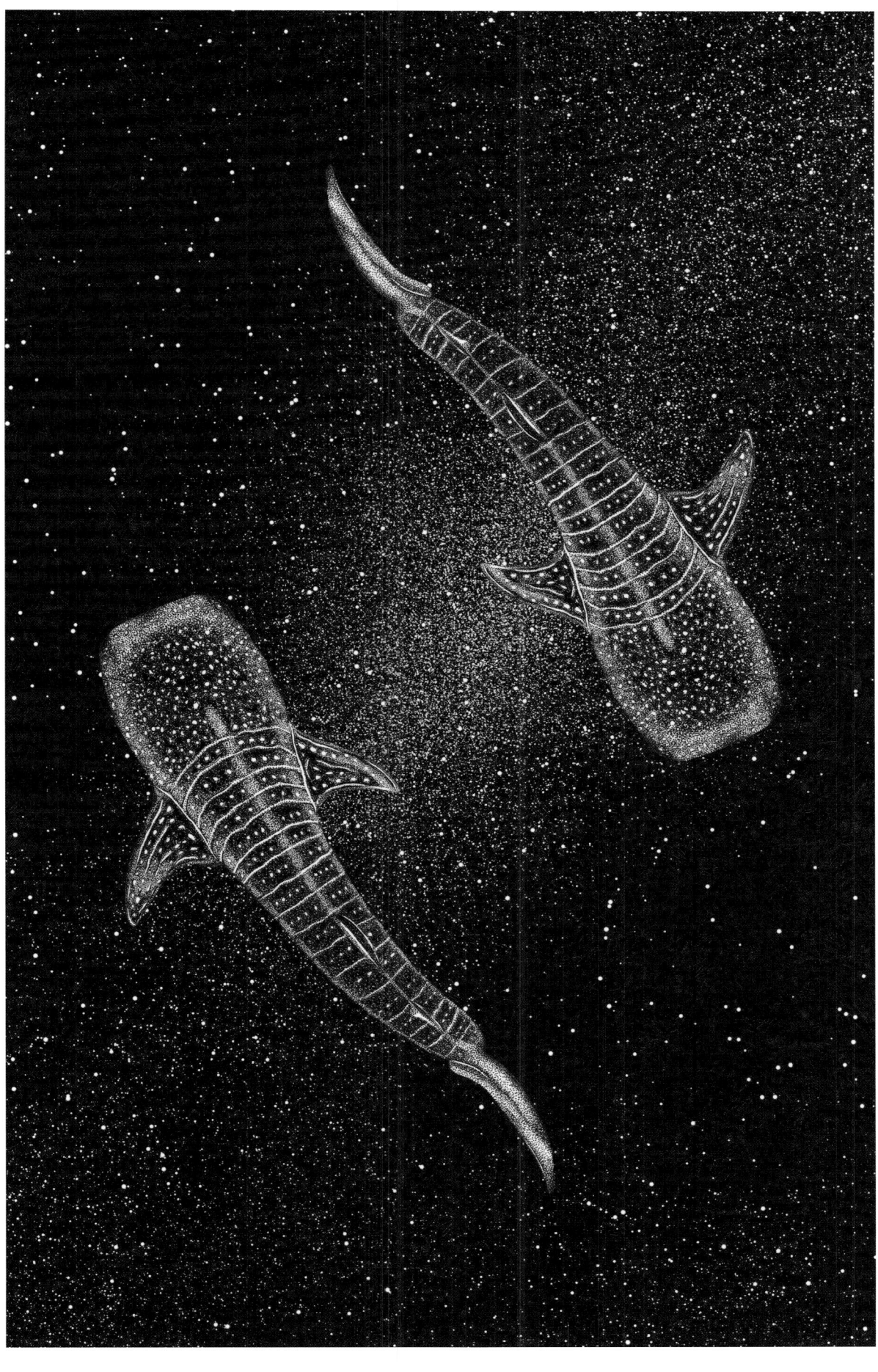

FOR BRIGHT MINDS

Who hasn't heard of the book *Jaws*? Or maybe you have seen the movie based on the book? It was directed by the famous Steven Spielberg, and it shows a shark as an ice-cold, almost demonic killer that relentlessly hunts helpless humans. What is not so well known is that the author of the book, and even Spielberg himself, have apologized many times for making people so afraid of sharks that they want to kill them. Spielberg has made it very clear that he deeply regrets the decimation of shark populations his film caused. And Peter Benchley, who wrote the book, even said that, knowing what he knows about sharks today, he would never write that book again.

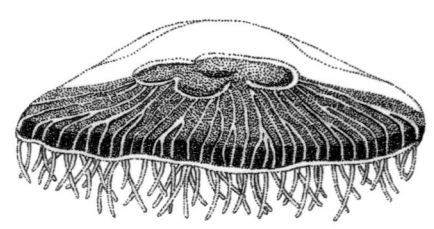

Simply put, the book and the film are absolute rubbish and have nothing to do with the real life of a great white shark. We get much more wisdom from the many island cultures, where sharks have always been worshipped and admired as gods. Hawaii, for example, is said to be home to a powerful shark god called Kāmohoaliʻi, who controls the weather and the ocean. In Fiji, the shark god Dakuwaqa is known for his ability to transform into a human—he is considered a fearless warrior. In the Cook Islands, people tell stories about the great King of the Sharks, Tekea, who once saved a beautiful maiden, the beloved of the God of the Ocean, from drowning. Age-old rock paintings by Aboriginal Australians immortalize sharks because they believe sharks played an important role in the world's creation.

The ancient Greeks, Chinese, Egyptians and Native Americans have many similar positive stories and legends. So let's pay more attention to these ancient traditions because it's high time we treated sharks with respect. I am therefore really happy that in November 2022, at the conference on the Washington Convention on International Trade in Endangered Species of Wild Fauna and Flora (CITES), 184 countries finally agreed to place around 100 shark species under protection. This means that they may only be hunted as long as their populations are not shrinking too much. That may not sound like a lot, but it is an incredible breakthrough!

Gold, Gold, Gold!

You may also find it worth your while to know everything about gold (for our teeth, for example). First, let me ask you (and your parents) the crucial question: do you know where gold comes from? Because it's odd: everyone, without exception, knows what gold is and how valuable it is, but hardly anyone knows how it was formed and where it came from. I've heard the most outlandish theories about this; many believe that gold is somehow generated in the ground, like diamonds, perhaps in volcanic vents, under very high pressure. Some believe that gold is a mixture of different chemical substances that "come together" in the rock to form gold veins. Others believe that gold is formed by water, which is why we find gold nuggets in rivers and streams. Right… I don't even know what to say to that. You better hold on tight. I'll come right out and say it: all the gold on our planet comes from outer space! It became part of our Earth when our planet was formed from cosmic dust, comets, liquid rock and other materials. Scientists agree that gold can only be created as a result of a supernova. That is the explosion of a massive star, much larger than our Sun. At least eight to ten times as big. Before such a supernova occurs, a previously "normal" star "mutates" into a so-called "neutron star". These are extremely condensed stars that only have a diameter of around twenty kilometres—and yet have much more mass than our Sun. Imagine if we were to squeeze our Sun like a sponge, making it as small as possible. That's what the universe does with some stars—and the result is a supernova.

I'm sure some bright minds will now want to know exactly how much mass our Sun has. All right: our Sun has a mass of 1.9891 octillion tonnes (an octillion is a one with twenty-seven zeros). That's actually pretty straightforward to calculate. But I can't really get my head around a number that big. An octillion certainly sounds like a frightening amount of mass. To give you an idea, that's equivalent to the mass of 332,946 Earths. Quite a lot of Earths, if you ask me. Now, if two of these neutron stars collide in space (like two cars crashing into each other), this can produce a lot of gold. Making gold requires an incredible amount of energy, which also explains why we cannot produce artificial gold on Earth (though we can make diamonds!). Incidentally, there is quite a lot of gold on Earth, but who knows, maybe there are billions and billions of other planets in the universe where a lot more of it could be found… we'll probably never know.

An estimated 200,000 tonnes of gold have been mined over the course of human history. That sounds like quite a lot of precious metal, but if you were to make all this gold into a single giant cube, it would only measure around twenty-two metres on each side. Remember, even the megalodon was longer than twenty-two metres! Do you want another example? OK, how about this: if you covered a football pitch with all the gold mined in the world to date, it would only form a layer 1.25 metres high. Most of you could stand right next to it and still look across it quite easily.

Earth has a lot more (inaccessible) gold in its core. Calculations suggest there are around 1.6 septillion tonnes (that's a one with twenty-four zeros!) of the metal that are beyond our reach. It's surely unthinkable that mankind would dare to fiddle with the core of our own planet. I've always found it fascinating that this extraterrestrial gold is the basis of our whole civilization. After all, all the money in the world was originally made up of gold and silver coins. Later, however, the banks started keeping the heavy coins in their vaults and issued banknotes instead (which were much easier and more practical to transport) but would retain their value… just like the actual gold and silver. That's how our money was created!

FOR BRIGHT MINDS

I want to reveal my absolute favourite massive number to you—the "octillion". As you know, my favourite normal number is seven. I told you about seven and why it is my favourite in *Amazing Jellyfish*, but there is something exciting about these huge, incredible numbers. Everyone will probably know the million. And maybe even the billion. But my favourite giant number, the octillion, is much better. That is because, if you ask me, it would also be the favourite number of an octopus. It's a truly enormous number, consisting of one followed by forty-eight(!) zeros. But there's another way to remember it: the word consists of two parts: "octi" + "llion". The "llion" comes from the word million. And we all know how many zeros there are in a million, don't we? 1,000,000. That's right, six. And "octi" always has something to do with the number eight. Do you remember? An octopus always has eight arms! And since 6 × 8 = 48, an octillion logically has forty-eight zeros. It looks like this:

1,000,000,000,000,000,000,000,000,000,000,000,000,000,000,000,000.

Mention this to your maths teacher at school—they'll be amazed by your knowledge! Although, if you're in the US, perhaps you'd better not say anything to your teacher, as over there this number is actually known as a quindecillion… (I know, right? Why does it have to be so complicated?!)

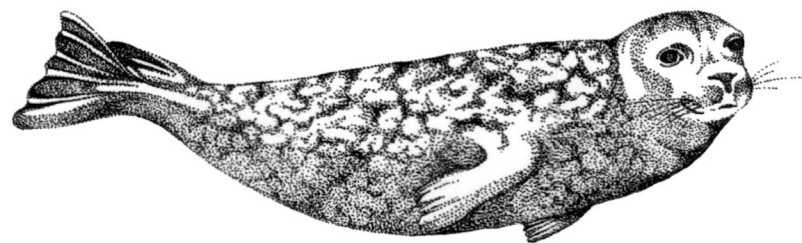

SEVEN TIMES FUN

1. How did the shark plead in court?
   Gill-ty!

2. Who is a shark's favourite Star Wars character?
   Chew-bacca!

3. Where was the first place the shark visited in Europe?
   Fin-land.

4. What's a shark's favourite card game?
   Go fish!

5. Why was the shark so funny?
   He was hilariously shark-astic.

6. Why do restaurant owners not like sharks?
   Because they always use up all the toothpicks.

7. How do sharks greet their buddies?
   Water you up to?

ICE-COLD SHARKS AND THE SECRETS OF THE SEAS

I thought long and hard about which shark species I would like to introduce because I realize that you are all shark experts. You're probably familiar with some of the more common and widespread species—great white sharks, hammerheads, tiger sharks and bull sharks.

So, I thought it would be more exciting to introduce you to some species you might not know. These sharks live under the ice and in cold water, where you can't easily observe them. And by cold water, I mean freezing water, where other warm-water sharks wouldn't dare to go and wouldn't survive. I'm particularly fond of these "ice-cold sharks" because they have some remarkable characteristics, but more on that in a moment.

The Secrets of the Seas

I don't think hard enough about many things—that's something really bright minds should be doing! Here's one of those things, for example: the Atlantic Ocean is getting bigger and bigger! It's like an inflating balloon (I'll admit it, the comparison is a bit of a stretch). And the Pacific Ocean, in turn, is getting smaller and smaller (like a deflating balloon). All this is happening because our continental plates (basically our continents) are moving.

The North American plate is continuously moving away from the European (actually Eurasian) plate, creating a crack thousands of kilometres long in the Atlantic Ocean floor that is spewing red-hot lava. It goes without saying that these plates move very slowly (snails move at Formula One speeds by comparison!) which is why we don't even notice it. It happens at the speed of... well, your fingernails growing (a few centimetres a year). In Iceland, you can actually see the crack on land. Presumably, one day, there will even be two Icelands?

"*Panta rhei*"—"everything flows"—is a famous phrase coined by the Greek philosopher Heraclitus, which means that everything in the world (and in the cosmos) is constantly changing and moving. Memorize this quote; you can show off how smart you are. Incidentally, I memorized this quote as a child with the help of a "mnemonic" device: panda + ray = panta rhei (that reminds me, I really must set you a challenge on mnemonic devices. I'll come back to that in a moment).

FOR BRIGHT MINDS

The mnemonic device I'm referring to is a reliable method to remember things you might forget. Recently, for example, I watched a crime series on TV starring a detective called "Monk", well, actually, he is an ex-detective and sometimes even an ex-ex-detective, but that's by the by). In one of the cases, he says the following sentence: "Big cousins eat fifteen pizzas." As it soon turns out, this is a mnemonic device for memorizing a car number plate, which reads BCE 15P. If I had seen a number plate like that, I would never have been able to memorize it. BUT: "Big cousins eat fifteen pizzas"? Anyone can remember that.

Ingenious. Mnemonic devices are handy memory tools. I'm sure your teachers sometimes work with them too, maybe even your music teacher? They could use the following mnemonic: "Every Amateur Does Get Better Eventually." E, A, D, G, B, E. This is an excellent way to memorize the arrangement of strings on a guitar. And now, of course, you have a little task: write down a car registration number you want to memorize and make your mnemonic for it, OK? If you have a lot of numbers, it's a good idea to link them with words that rhyme; I guarantee you it will work with a bit of practice. And if not, it's still fun! And to set a good example, here's an imaginary registration: TB88 AMD (and if it exists, sorry, that was pure coincidence!). My mnemonic for it is: "This bridge ate! Ate all my donkeys." Now it's your turn!

_____

_____

_____

Did you know that, ages ago, all the land on our planet was formed into a single supercontinent? We call it "Pangaea", which comes from Greek and means "land of everything". Pangaea was a vast land mass that formed roughly 275 million years ago, and then, around 175 million years ago, this whole Pangaea mass began to break apart, and the continents, as we know them today, drifted off to where they are now.

They're still moving, at much-less-than-a-snail's pace, as I said, and supposedly they will drift together again one day to form another supercontinent…

Fascinating, isn't it? There will be no more America, Africa or Europe. We will all be Pangaeans again. Or whatever word they come up with. The Earth will look completely different.

This will also, among other things, impact our ocean currents. One of the most critical phenomena in the sea is the "Gulf Stream". It is a massive ocean current in the Atlantic Ocean that transports 150 million cubic metres of warmer water towards Europe every second! That means the Gulf Stream transports 100 times as much water as all the world's rivers. Mind-boggling. And the Gulf Stream is essential for our climate! Without it, Europe would be five to ten degrees colder, which would be particularly challenging for farming. And that means also for our food supply.

Another thing I don't think about enough is the fact that there are huge underwater meadows in the ocean! The most widespread seaweed is called "Neptune grass", named after the Roman god of the seas. It is also one of the oldest known organisms on earth. A genetic study recently showed that the seagrass meadows off the coast of Spain, for example, could be around 100,000 years old. That is definitely older than Grandpa. And this seagrass provides an extremely important habitat for many marine animals—we'll return to that later.

It is a relatively open secret that I like mountains on, in and under the sea. If someone asked me which is the highest mountain in the world, I would answer without hesitation: Mount Everest. But that's wrong because Mauna Kea in Hawaii is over 10,000 metres high. Only around 4,200 metres of it are visible above the surface—the rest of the mountain is underwater. I still think that counts, though, don't you? After all, a mountain is a mountain! And while we're at it, do you know the highest mountain in our solar system? It's called Olympus Mons, and it's on Mars. It rises an incredible 22,000 metres into the sky, and its circumference (the base) is almost the size of Germany.

By the way, since we are talking about underwater mountains, we should mention the mysterious "black smokers", which can rise as high as fifty metres from the seabed. These are like large chimneys spewing out black clouds, and many scientists

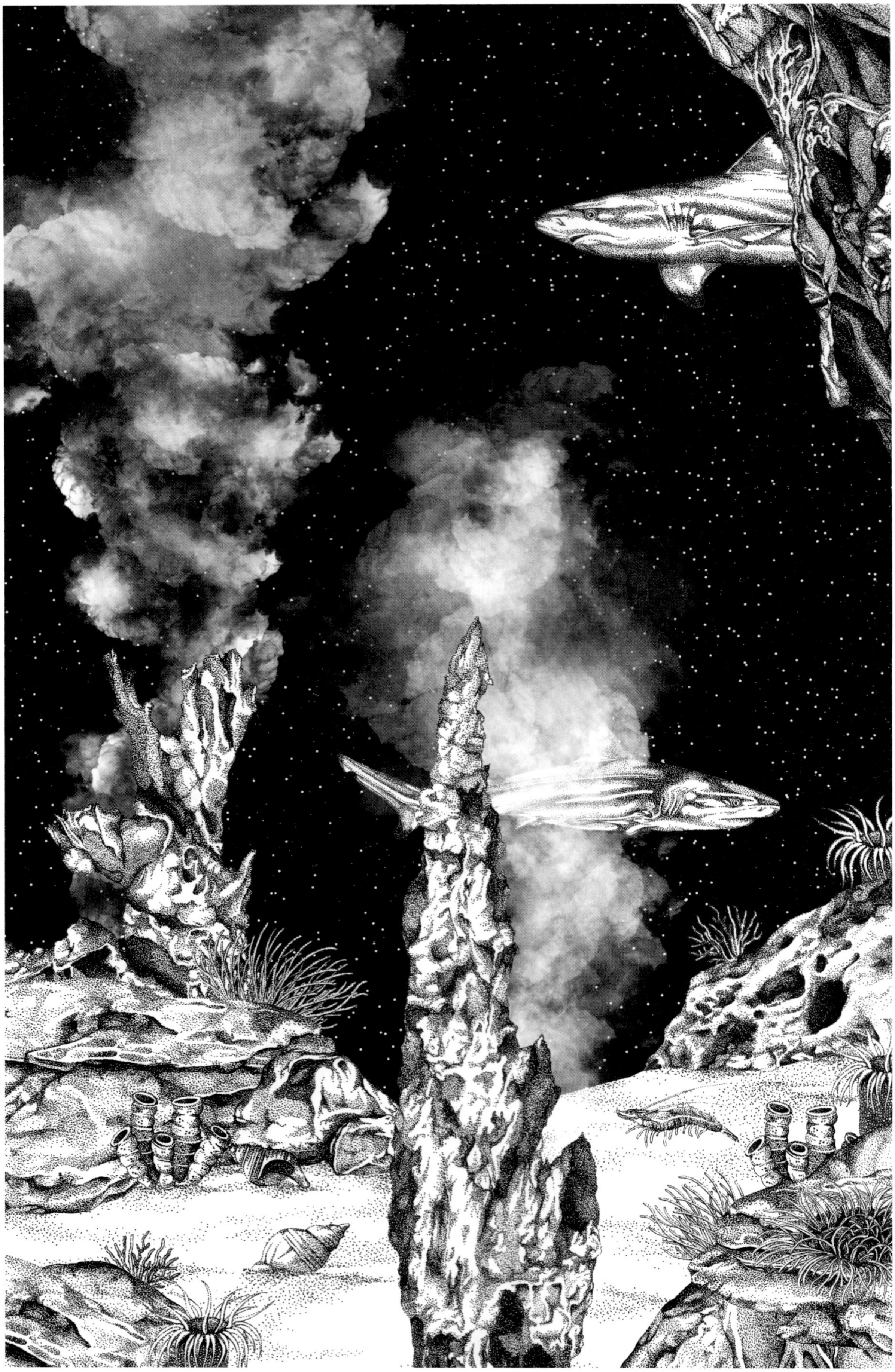

argue life on Earth likely began near one of them—not in the shallow water many other researchers are betting on. Well, I have no idea how and where life began, but we should not ignore these black smokers.

And do you know what freedivers are? They are people who dive without air tanks. While they can, of course, also dive in lakes, ponds or bathtubs, they find the sea more exciting. Freedivers hold their breath for a very long time. Get this: Croatian freediver Budimir Šobat, the current record holder, can hold his breath for twenty-four minutes and thirty-seven seconds. He's officially listed in *The Guinness Book of Records*. I can't even manage a minute. Unbelievable. But my favourite freediver by far is Julie Gautier. Would you like to see her short film about diving and dancing? It's called *Ama*, and you'll find a link to it at the end of the book.

The Sharks Who Came in from the Cold

I used to think sharks lived only in tropical and temperate seas—but never in the Arctic, close to the North Pole, with polar bears and the like. I was wrong because a few shark species actually like icy water.

Yet hardly any sharks are regularly observed near the Antarctic (i.e. the South Pole). Spiny dogfish (also known as mud sharks) are said to pop by there from time to time, and even great white sharks occasionally visit the cold regions of the Arctic and Antarctic, but these have been the exception so far. If we were to travel back in time—let's say a mere 40 million years—we would encounter a completely different ocean near the South Pole: warm tropical water. Paleobiologist Jürgen Kriwet, from the University of Vienna, has identified twenty-four shark species that once lived around the Antarctic. As we see again, the geology and climate of our planet are constantly changing.

The most prominent shark in the Arctic is the Greenland shark. It looks different from the sharks we are used to seeing. I have to say: the Greenland shark is a cool dog!

Sharks can live to be relatively old (between fifteen and fifty years on average), but that's nothing compared to the incredible

Greenland shark, which can live for 400 to 500 years or more. Isn't that just extraordinary? Science attributes its almost biblical longevity to its slow movements. Its metabolism is always just "ticking over", and even its heart beats only once every ten seconds. Check your watch—ten seconds is longer than you think. Incidentally, the Greenland shark's scientific name is *Somniosus microcephalus*—the first part of which means "the sleeping one" or "the dreamer", and the larger an individual is, the older it is (makes sense!). There have been sightings of Greenland sharks that were as much as eight metres long. That's quite a chunk. Their stomachs have been found to contain the remains of seals and even polar bears, which suggests that Greenland sharks may be more active and more formidable hunters than we realized.

Another shark that lives in icy seas seems to go more for the thorny look, with a spike on each of its dorsal fins. So, there's not much mystery about how the spiny dogfish (*Squalus acanthias*) got its name. The spines are an additional defence. They can be quite painful if touched (the shark has venom glands there!) and are clearly intended to ward off enemies.

And the spiny dogfish shark, which is usually only one metre long, does have a lot of enemies. It gets hunted by larger sharks, killer whales and seals. But it is us humans who have hunted it almost to extinction. We catch this animal in such large numbers that its population cannot recover. To make it worse,

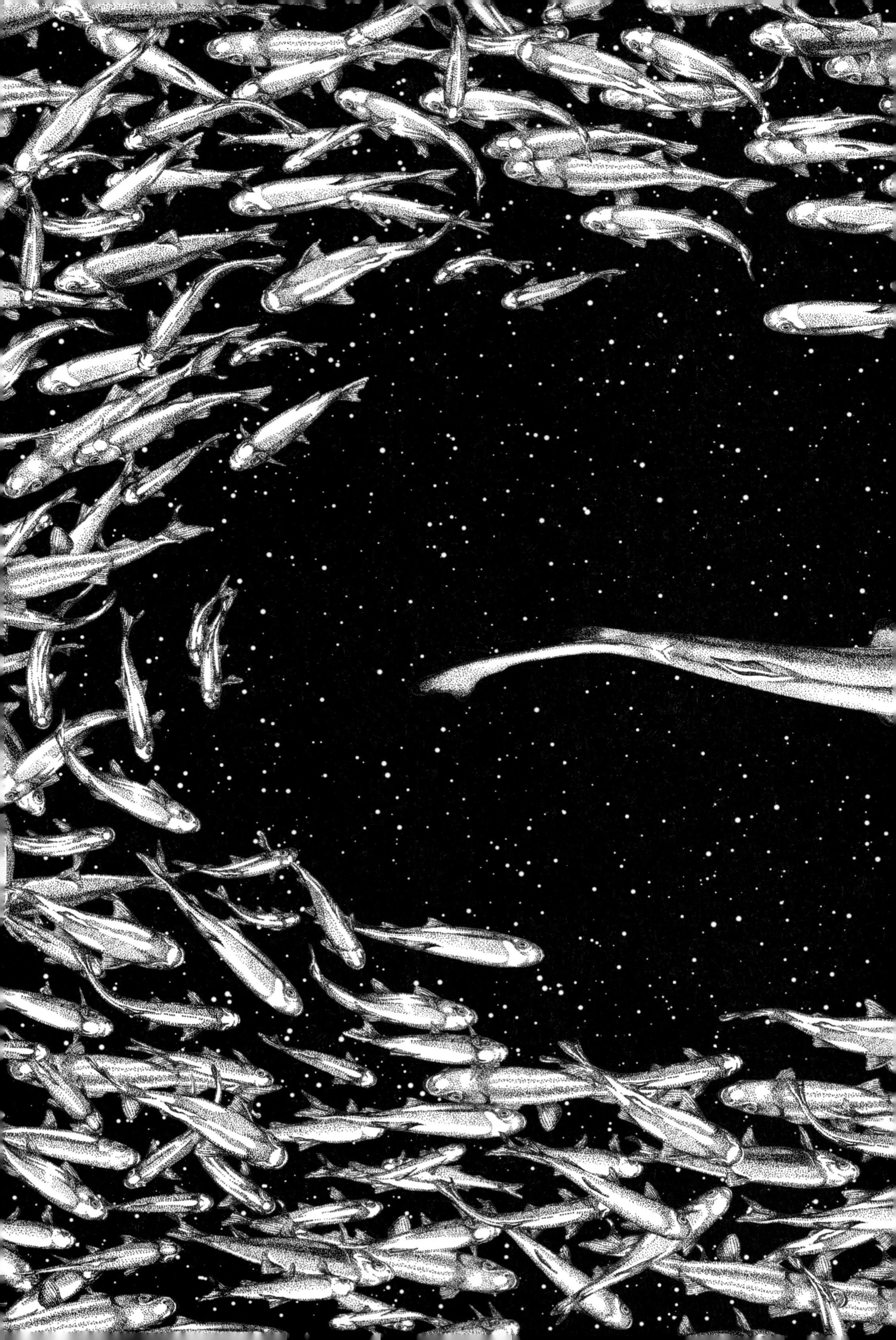

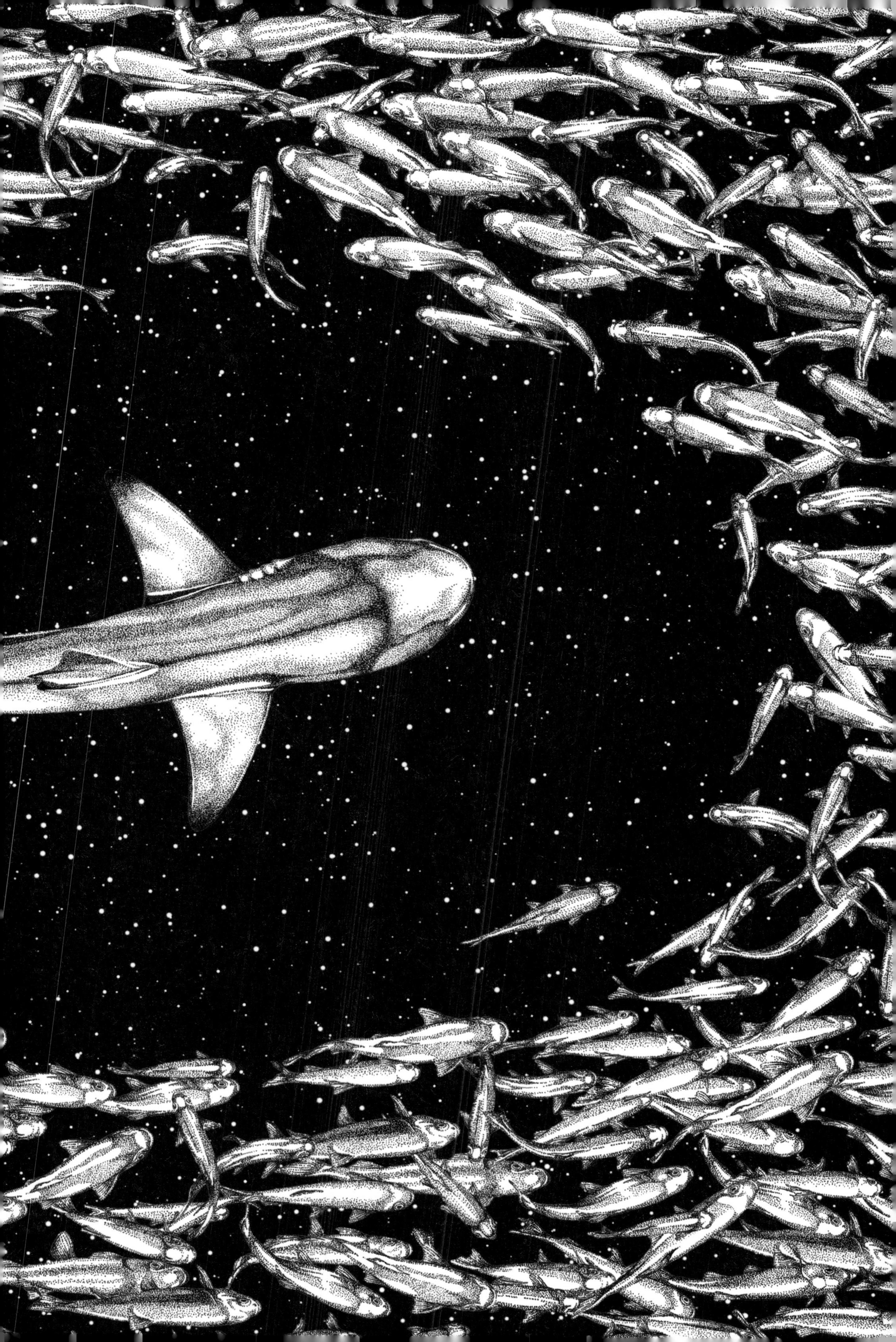

female spiny dogfish sharks can only reproduce after fifteen to twenty years. For this shark species, which used to be quite common (the animals live in tropical and polar seas), the horrible story can be documented with numbers: in the 1980s, up to 50,000 tonnes of them were being caught per year; in 2007 only 2,500 tonnes were caught. If we continue like this, there will soon be no more spiny dogfish at all.

Here's something really important for all you bright minds, so listen up: you should never eat shark meat. Sadly, this does happen far too much, and I'll tell you about that later. But what makes me really sad is that the spiny dogfish shark is also on the menu here in Europe, and we must stop that! The tricky thing is that it does not appear on menus or in shops under its own name; no, the actual identity of the animal is deliberately concealed. In Germany it is called "*Schillerlocke*" (because it looks like the long "locks" or hair of the German poet Friedrich Schiller). Most Germans who buy it don't know they're eating shark. They think it's cod or pollock.

So, "*Schillerlocke*" in Germany is in fact spiny dogfish, and the British aren't much better, I'm afraid! If you've ever seen "rock salmon" on the menu when ordering fish and chips, that could have been spiny dogfish too. (It's just a marketing name to make the fish sound tastier—it has nothing to do with salmon!) So much for the British national dish. Hardly anyone realizes that they are eating shark meat because of these naming tricks.

Isn't it absolutely terrible? The poor spiny dogfish (which, as I said, is threatened with extinction) is disguised with other names so that people will continue to eat it. There are many more such names for fish in English that are intended to hide from customers that they are eating sharks: catfish, greyfish, whitefish, steakfish, lemonfish, smoked dogfish—all of which are spiny dogfish sharks.

Just imagine some other animal you would never eat—a crow, for example—being sold as "black chicken", "moon quail" or "night pheasant". I think that's a massive cheat, and we should all question what we're being sold or served.

How Humans are a Threat to Sharks Everywhere

No matter where sharks live, they are almost always in mortal danger, and we humans are the ones endangering them. Over time, we have spread so much fear that we are depriving all larger predators of their right to exist. Wolves, tigers, jaguars, lions, polar bears… the list is long. Speaking of lists, there is a well-known Red List of Threatened Species where you can check which animals are threatened with extinction worldwide.

Exactly twenty-eight per cent of all animal species on our planet are threatened with extinction. That means they are almost gone—forever. However, this percentage does not even include species that we have already driven to extinction. According to the renowned German news magazine *Der Spiegel*, up to 58,000 animal species become extinct every year (there are thought to be around 8 million animal species in total). Let that sink in—we lose that many species every year forever. We cannot accept this any longer!

Unfortunately, this terrible trend also affects almost all shark species, which is an utter catastrophe. A world without sharks would be like not having a single lion, tiger or leopard left on the planet. Sharks (and all other apex predators) are essential for intact ecosystems, and I can assure you that an ocean without sharks will not work. I will tell you more about this in another chapter.

The International Fund for Animal Welfare (IFAW) estimates that humans kill around 100 million sharks per year, or more precisely, 274,000 every single day. That's three sharks per second. These facts should make all of us cry out in rage. According to Hai-Swiss (a foundation in Switzerland), almost 1.5 million tonnes of sharks are caught by humans for their meat and especially their fins. But many are caught and killed only to be processed into fishmeal, which is truly gross. People add fishmeal to all kinds of animal feed, such as for cattle and

AMAZING SHARK

49

Grab your crayons—this picture needs a lot of colour! Do you dare?

sheep farming. So our hamburgers are made from cows fed with ground-up sharks. Honestly? I think that's completely sick. Don't you?

Asia, in particular, poses a huge problem for shark populations because that is where shark fins are much in demand. Have you ever heard of shark-fin soup? Clearly, you shouldn't order it anywhere, but many diners in Asia don't seem to care. Shark-fin soup is considered to be very healthy, and sharks as "medicine" are also quite popular there. For example, there is a myth that sharks don't get cancer and so people can be cured of cancer if they eat enough shark meat. This is, of course, complete nonsense; there are around forty known types of cancer in sharks. In Hong Kong, by the way, a soup made from a certain kind of shark will cost you around £400, which shows just how much money can be made from killing sharks.

When I see how the shark fins are "harvested", I am overcome with horror. Unfortunately, my dear, bright minds, I can't spare you in this chapter. You have to know about these practices to help the sharks. This whole process is called "finning": long lines with baited hooks are laid out in the ocean. They can be around 130 kilometres long! These are used to catch sharks en masse, which are then pulled onboard the ships. There, their fins are cut off while they are still alive, and the mutilated animal is thrown back into the water alive. The sharks die slowly since they can't swim without their fins. If you ask me, this is one of the cruellest things you can do. According to the organization Pro Wildlife, around 70 million sharks die this way every year.

CHAPTER 03

THE FAST AND THE GLORIOUS
—SHARK EDITION—

One of the first sea creatures I came across as a child, and which I still find fascinating today, was the so-called "flying fish". I was convinced at the time that my mother must have made them up because: why would fish fly? Birds fly. Full stop. And the only mammal that can fly is the bat, or so I thought. And by the way, did you know that two-thirds of the mammals on our planet are bats? Bats even outnumber rodents, as in mice and rats and the like. Incredible but true: there are more than 1,400 bat species on this planet!

Now, I would like to introduce you to the most curious flying animals that I have come across so far:

1. A frog that sails through the air? Here it is: Wallace's flying frog (it bears the name of the revered British naturalist Alfred Russel Wallace). It's more of a short-distance glider, usually from one tree to the next.

2. Have you ever heard of the sugar glider? It has its own flight membrane—thin skin connecting its front and back legs, so when it spreads all its legs out, it almost looks like a bat. This allows it to glide up to sixty metres. It's adorable and fits in a child's hand—that's how tiny it is.

3. Do you want to meet a flying snake? Voilà, here's the paradise flying snake which can spread its ribs so wide that it can glide up to twenty metres.

4. Have you ever encountered the common flying dragon? Don't let the word "common" fool you—there's nothing ordinary about this one! In fact, I believe these common flying dragons are quite special. Without a doubt, they're the most unusual lizards you'll ever encounter. And guess what? They can also glide with their very own flight membranes. Isn't that amazing?

When I was a child, I wasn't aware of all of these amazing facts. I did know that sometimes fish jumped out of water, which I loved watching in our local ponds. However, discovering that flying fish burst out of the water, spread their wing-like fins, and glided across the sea was a delightful surprise to me.

When I first saw photographs of flying fish, I thought they were fantasy creatures! But it made more sense once I learnt that these amazing animals actually flee from predators by gliding through the air. Isn't that clever? These fish can really cover some distance—up to half a kilometre! Like skipping stones, they can also bounce off the water's surface to take flight again. Do you remember finding a perfect flat stone and seeing how many skips you could get on the water? Just so you know, the world record for skipping stones is eighty-eight bounces,

AMAZING SHARK 55

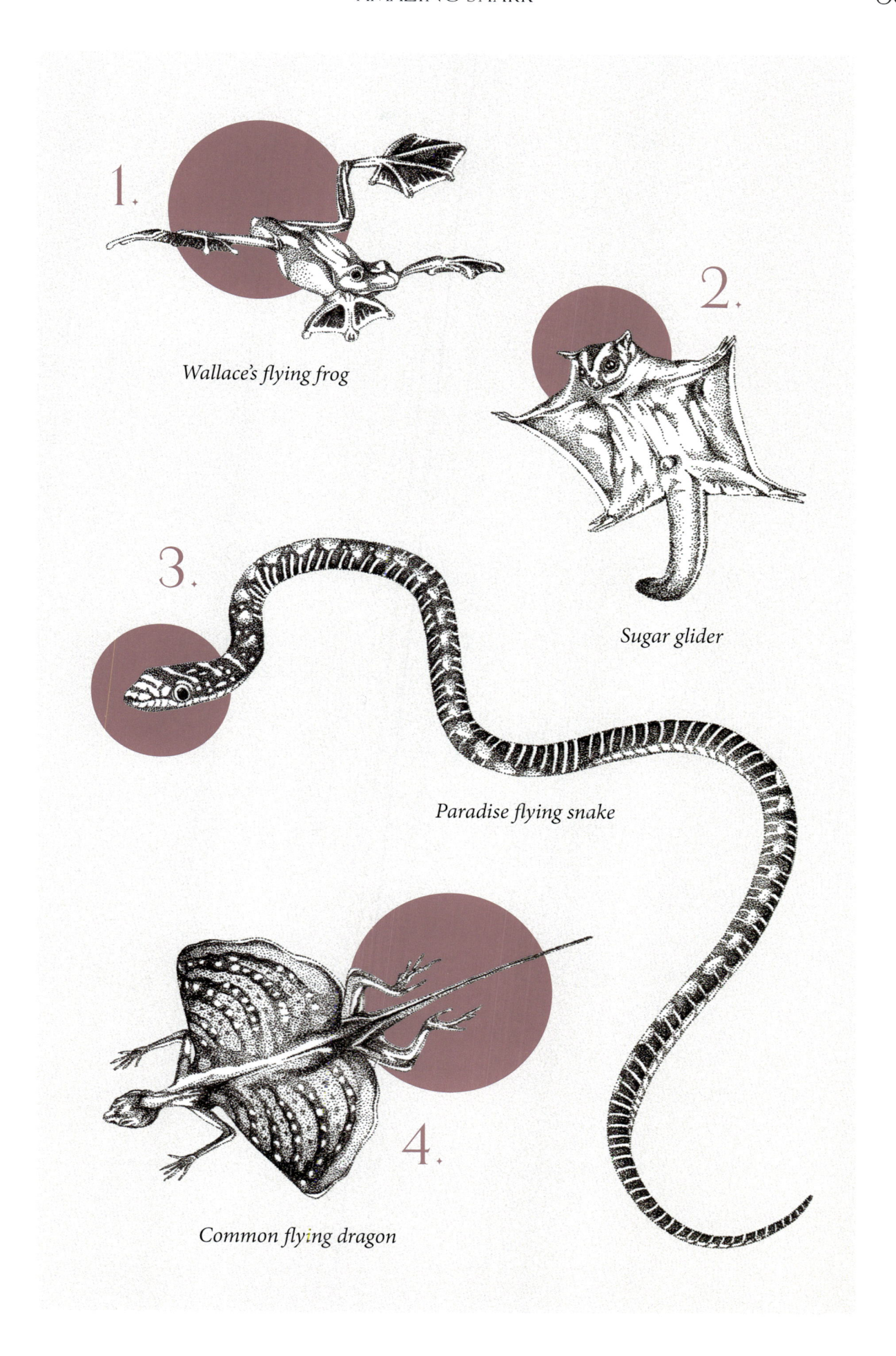

1. Wallace's flying frog

2. Sugar glider

3. Paradise flying snake

4. Common flying dragon

reaching almost 100 metres. Looks like you have to put in quite a bit of practice if you want to break that record!

Let's take a closer peek at one of these flying fish. Isn't it just so adorable? And doesn't it remind you of a strange bird? For the longest time, I really wanted an aquarium full of flying fish that would occasionally take a spin around the living room before diving back into the water.

Flying fish launch themselves out of the water with a mighty leap! They glide through the air without flapping their fins, making them more like gliders than birds. They can reach incredible speeds of about seventy kilometres per hour and soar up to five metres above the water. Some flying fish can grow up to forty-five centimetres in size. There are quite a few species of them (around fifty-two). I can't go into more detail right now, but if you're interested, you can do your own research.

I'm sure you bright minds are already thinking: Michael, you started this section of the book with the title "The Fast and The Beautiful—Shark Edition" and now we're talking about flying fish? What's that all about? Yes, I've also been thinking—oh dear, it really is high time I introduced you to this special shark.

The shark I am talking about is the great white! Great whites are special because they can catapult themselves out of the water like flying fish. However, in their case, they are not escaping predators but are on the hunt themselves. Great white sharks obviously can't glide above the water. But because they are such huge and majestic animals, their leaps are all the more memorable. Between you and me, other jumping sea creatures (whales, dolphins and the like) are nothing compared to these extraordinary acrobats.

I remember when I first saw a documentary about this on TV. I could not believe what I saw. A great white shark, over five metres long, shot out of the water like a rocket while I sat wide-eyed in front of the television. It's one of the most impressive things I've ever seen in the animal kingdom. And, as it turns out, it is not common behaviour for great whites. There are only a few places where these acrobatic leaps can be observed regularly, such as in False Bay on Seal Island in South Africa. This has turned the local great white sharks there into real stars.

Photographer Chris Fallows has documented the record jump of a great white shark. The animal leapt almost 3.7 metres out of the water. Oh, I would love to have been there, wouldn't you?

I have read that some shark species also jump when they want to communicate with other creatures or generally draw attention to themselves (the basking shark was mentioned

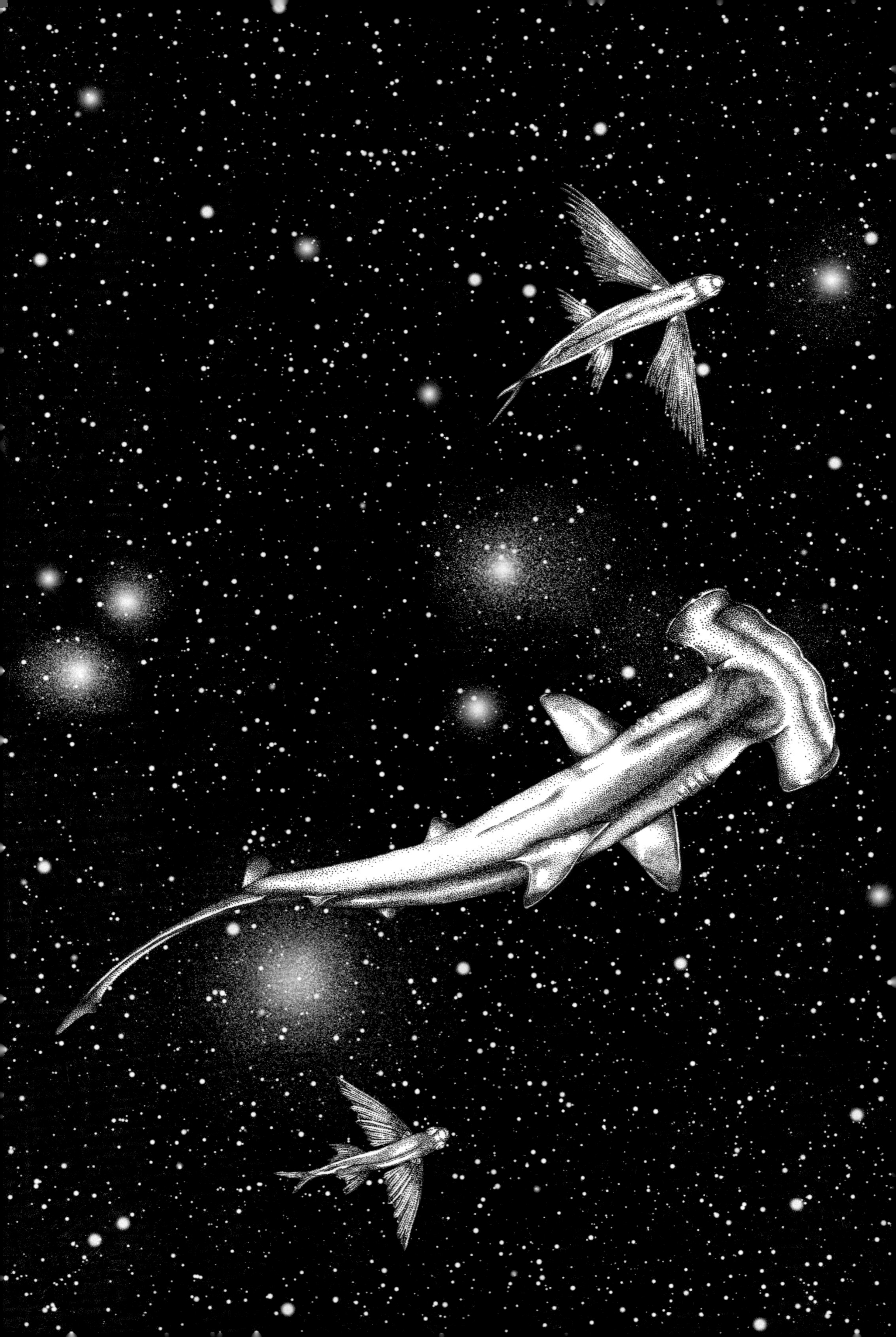

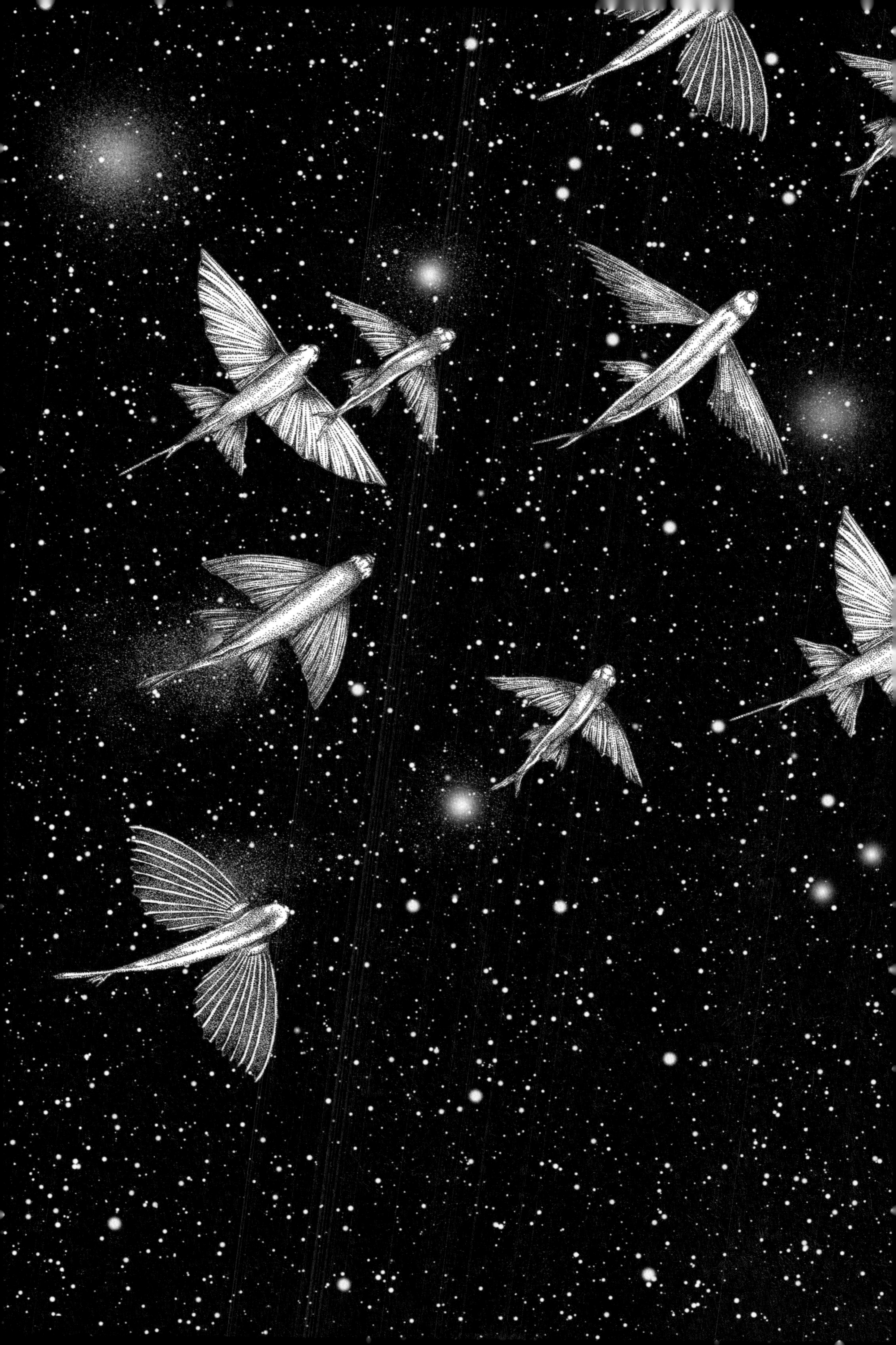

as an example, and I will write about it later). This would make sharks similar to whales, who exhibit this behaviour daily. Research shows that whales mainly jump out of the water (and drop back with a huge splash) when the whales they want to communicate with are far away. If the whales are closer, humpback whales, for example, will slap the water with their mighty flukes. Perhaps this is a polite greeting? The absolute high-jump world champions are, of course, the dolphins—they can actually jump up to seven metres out of the water.

As I know all my bright minds quite well by now, I can literally hear the questions out there in the background: Michael! Which land mammal jumps the highest? The answer is really clear in this case… it's the puma! The cougar/mountain lion/panther (all different names for the puma) can jump up to six metres high. From a standing start! No other animal in the world can do it.

But when we talk about the long jump, we must recognize that although the flea is not a mammal, its jumping power is truly enormous in relation to its size. Remember that the average flea is just three millimetres long and can leap over 200 times its own body length. That's roughly 60 centimetres! That doesn't sound like a lot, but let us apply that to the cougar, which can grow to between 2 and 2.4 metres in length. Let's keep the calculation simple: 2 metres x 200? Yes, that's

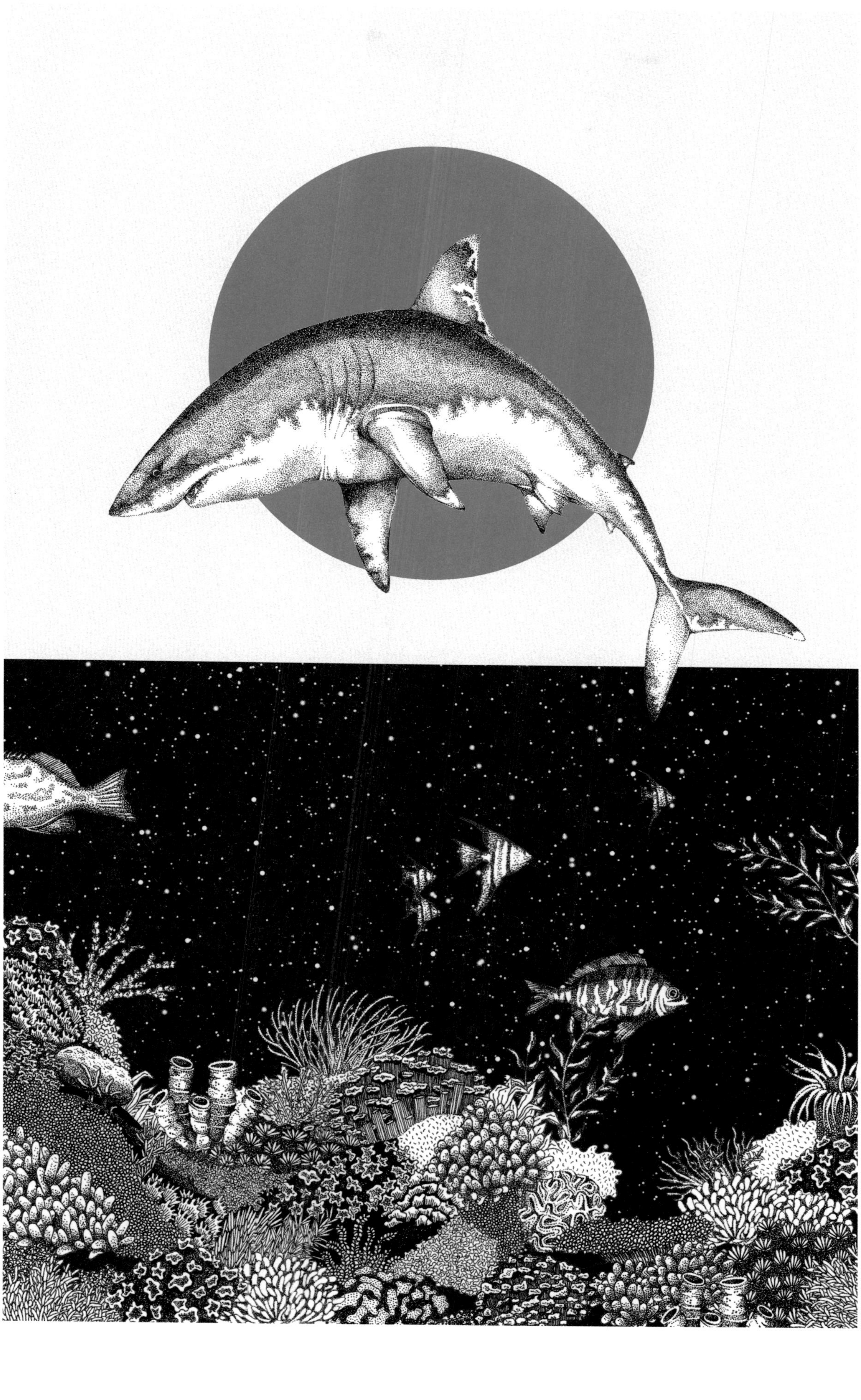

how far the cougar would have to jump to compete with the flea. That's unbelievable, isn't it? How tall are you, and how far could you jump if you were a flea? (Just multiply your height by 200).

Shark Quiz

I've devised a shark challenge for you that I hope you can solve. It has nothing to do with high jumps or long jumps, but it will finally allow me to introduce you to my absolute favourite sharks! Drum roll! So, while I gather them, you can solve this not-so-easy puzzle.

SHARK QUIZ

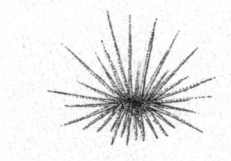

Which of the following shark species really exist—and which have I just made up? You have to decide! (*Answers on p. 133*)

1. Carpet shark or curtain shark?
2. Apple shark or lemon shark?
3. Bamboo shark or birch shark?

What? Are you saying these were too easy? Do you want harder ones? Fine…

4. Common badger shark, false catshark or spotted agaric shark?
5. Bignose shark, smoothskin shark or smallmouth shark?
6. Seychelles shark, Corsica shark or Galapagos shark?
7. Argentine screw shark, Japanese saw shark or Indian plier shark?
8. Crocodile shark, hyena shark or gorilla shark?

Now what? Do you want it even more difficult? You bright minds really are tough! I'm proud of you. Well, here we go:

9. Prickly dogfish, shady seagoat or stripy oceancat?
10. Pacific sleeper shark, Atlantic nap shark or Northern Pacific break shark?
11. Pillow shark, pyjama shark or duvet shark?

Amazing—so many strange shark species, and we've managed to give them equally strange names. But before I introduce you to my favourite sharks, perhaps I'll take a short nap. That's one of the things that sets us apart from sharks, by the way, because most of them never truly sleep. Sometimes they will enter a relaxed state, although still swimming slowly along with their eyes open, but that's as close as they get to catching forty winks. Many sharks also have to move constantly otherwise they would die, because they don't get enough oxygen flowing through their gills. A few shark species can make themselves comfortable at the bottom of the ocean, but not for very long.

Just imagine if we had to keep moving all the time to breathe. Phew, that would be really exhausting. Especially when watching TV. And then we'd never be able to sleep again. I'm a little glad I don't have to be a shark.

Psst, and what's the best way to wake Michael up? You have a choice:

1. stuff chocolate in his mouth
2. tickle him
3. hold a meatloaf under his nose

To those who picked 2, I can only say: please, no!

My All-Time Top 11 Sharks!

1. **The zebra shark** (*Stegostoma tigrinum*): I must confess I love zebras. They always cheer me up. Perhaps it's their cheeky stripes? Those stripes help the animals to repel insects, by the way. Totally cool! Somehow, flies and other insects don't like stripy patterns. To test this idea, researchers once disguised horses as zebras, and they were bitten and stung much less. Ingenious, right?

    And yes, there is a real zebra shark, an aquatic zebra in the flesh! It is also called a leopard shark because as it grows older, its markings turn into dark spots, but when it's young, it has smart stripes. Zebra sharks grow to around 2—2.5 metres in length, are harmless to us and prefer to feed on molluscs such as mussels and the like, which they suck out of their shells with relish. I secretly believe that zebra sharks invented oyster slurping! What? Never had oysters? Then ask your parents if they've ever eaten them. And where do zebra sharks actually live? In the Red Sea and the Pacific, for example.

2. **The shortfin mako** (*Isurus oxyrinchus*): This is a truly special fish, as it is believed to be the fastest shark and can accelerate to speeds of up to eighty kilometres per hour. Achieving that kind of speed underwater is not easy! This ability makes it possible to hunt some of the

fastest fish in the oceans, such as the bluefin tuna. The absolute fastest fish in the ocean are the black marlin and the famous sailfish (you've probably heard of it!). The former can reach a top speed of eighty kilometres per hour, while the latter can go even faster at 110 kilometres per hour. Those are motorway speeds! Incidentally, the short-finned mako can also catapult itself out of the water and reach heights of up to six metres above the surface, which is only slightly less than the record jumps of dolphins. It grows to a good four metres in length and weighs 500 kilograms (which is a lot). This species of shark is widespread. It can be found in the Mediterranean, off Norway, the British Isles and even in South Africa. However, shortfin mako are dwindling rapidly, and they are now listed as endangered. To me, these sharks are really special. And yes, there is also a long-finned mako (*Isurus paucus*). A "mid-fin mako" has not yet been discovered, but who knows…

3. **The goblin shark** (*Mitsukurina owstoni*): Have you ever heard of this strange-looking shark? I first encountered it not so long ago in an exciting documentary about deep-sea animals. I was immediately fascinated by its appearance because it looks more "alien" than other sharks. I've also often been told that I'm a cheeky goblin—so it's no wonder I like goblin sharks. It's practically a point of honour. This shark's long snout is definitely a special feature, and its

skin is a flesh-like, pale pink colour through which you can see its blood vessels. I read that this shark may be able to absorb oxygen through its skin, something that jellyfish, for example, can also do. As it lives at great depths, this ability would provide a considerable evolutionary advantage. The goblin shark has a large liver, which takes up around twenty-five per cent of its body. Scientists think that this enables the animals to go without food for a very long time, which is also very useful in the deep sea. These sharks usually grow up to four metres long, but in 2000, one specimen was discovered that was more than six metres. Quite an oversized goblin, then. It also uses its strange snout like a metal detector. It swims slowly across the seabed to detect its prey (I'll tell you more about that later) and its jaws can shoot forward. Its appearance is so unusual that a creature from one of the world-famous *Alien* films (*Alien: Covenant*) was given the jaws of the goblin shark. Of course, deep-sea and marine creatures have long provided inspiration for many filmmakers for their fantasy animals and monsters. However, they are not monsters and, apart from their looks, have nothing in common with these movie creatures!

4. **The frilled shark** (*Chlamydoselachus anguineus*): This one also looks like it came from another planet. Like the goblin shark, it lives in the deep sea. At first glance, it could be mistaken for a different fish. It has an elongated

body, almost like an eel or a python. These sharks grow to a length of two metres, and a study by Japanese scientists suggests that they have a gestation period of at least three and a half years. In other words, that's how long it takes for baby collar sharks to be born (two to twelve pups at a time). If this is true, it would be the longest gestation period of any vertebrate species known to us and about twice as long as the elephant's. As the species has not changed over the past 95 million years, the animals are also considered "living fossils" (a fossil is actually a fossilized, long-extinct creature from prehistoric times). We humans are particularly amazed when we come across such old animal species. I can remember, for example, watching a television documentary about the coelacanth, which was thought to be extinct and was suddenly rediscovered in 1938 in the deep sea off Madagascar. This fish is considered a close relative to the ancestors of all land animals because its fins enable it to perform a kind of "four-legged walk" underwater. Isn't that curious?

5. **The megamouth shark** (*Megachasma pelagios*): The megamouth shark is truly a jewel of the ocean. I can't help but be amazed by it. Alongside the whale shark and the basking shark, this is the only known shark species that feasts on tiny microorganisms like krill. Until 1976, the megamouth shark was a complete mystery to the world, even though it's far from small. Appropriately

named "megamouth", they can grow up to about six metres long. This fascinating species also resides in the deep sea, and by now, you may have caught on to the fact that I love deep-sea creatures. They are so strange, mysterious and wrapped in legend. Who knows what other incredible discoveries lie in wait down there at the bottom of the ocean? It is such a hard-to-reach environment that even massive animals can stay hidden. Could there be more colossal deep-sea sharks out there? The megamouth shark kind of reminds me of a giant tadpole, probably because its mouth makes up about twenty-two per cent of its body. That's pretty impressive.

6. **The blue shark** (*Prionace glauca*): I encountered my first favourite shark as a child in an animal encyclopaedia—it was the blue shark. I was so enchanted by its shimmering blue skin, its slender shape, its large (and in my opinion) friendly eyes and its graceful movements that I thought there couldn't be a more elegant and effortless swimmer. These sharks glide weightlessly through the water, and their agility puts even a hare to shame. Blue sharks live to be around twenty years old. They are considered "deep-sea sharks" because they're most comfortable in the open ocean. Blue sharks can cover astonishing distances: Marine biologists once tagged a blue shark that travelled 12,000 kilometres, swimming from New Zealand to Chile in a perfectly straight line. Incidentally, swimming on

70   THE FAST AND THE GLORIOUS

1.

Zebra shark

3.

2.

Shortfin mako

4.

Frilled shark

Thresher shark / fox shark

5.

Megamouth shark

9.

Salmon shark

AMAZING SHARK 71

Goblin shark

7.

Chain catshark

6.

Blue shark

8.

11.

Blacktip reef shark

10.

Dwarf lanternshark

such a straight course is not something most marine animals do. Besides the blue shark, only the tiger shark and the hammerhead shark have also been found to do this. Blue sharks can do this because they use the Earth's magnetic field to navigate. They are also thought to be able to sense the weak magnetic fields that many marine animals generate with their bodies—and that's how they hunt them. Like many other shark species, blue sharks orientate themselves by undersea mountain ranges. They basically have maps of the ocean floor in their heads—isn't that fascinating?

One of the largest known specimens of a blue shark ever found was around four metres long. The species is also thought to prefer to swim clockwise around the Earth! I wonder what that is all about?

7. **The chain catshark** (*Scyliorhinus retifer*): The chain catshark got its name because of the chain-like patterns on its skin. It likes to stay on the rocky seabed and lives mainly in the north-west Atlantic, for example, in the Caribbean. And here's why it's one of my favourite sharks: it can glow green! Unfortunately, we can only see this glow with special cameras, which is why researchers only recently discovered this phenomenon. But there are plenty of other animals in the water that glow. This property is called either "bio-fluorescence" (triggered by light) or

"bioluminescence" (produced by chemical reactions or enzymes). In any case, when blue light (of which there is plenty in the ocean) hits our chain catshark, it glows green. This is quite unique among sharks, and scientists suspect it helps them recognize and identify each other underwater. It seems that only they can see each other's magnificent green glow. It almost sounds like a superhero power, doesn't it? There is also the theory that the green glow helps to keep various microbes (microscopic creatures such as bacteria) away, which helps to keep the sharks in perfect health. I would love to glow green, especially if it meant I would never get sick again!

8. **The thresher shark** (*Alopias*): This group of sharks are also called fox sharks. Isn't this one truly beautiful? A gorgeous "underwater fox"? It is also the shark with the most beautiful tail fin! But tastes differ, after all, so let's stick to the facts: it is the shark with the longest tail fin in relation to its body. No wonder then that we "landlubbers" compare this shark to the fox, which also has a beautiful long tail. We know of three types of thresher shark: the **Pacific thresher shark**, the **bigeye thresher shark** (there is no small-eyed thresher shark) and the **common thresher shark**.

In the animal kingdom, "common" does not mean that an animal is somehow "vulgar". Scientists use this word in the sense of "ordinary". But if you ask me, a magnificent thresher shark could never be ordinary. A thresher shark can actually grow up to 7.5 metres long. That's quite something! The thresher shark is also one of those sharks that can jump high out of the water thanks to its long fin (which then works like a spring). Incidentally, it uses this fin to hunt fish; it whips (or "threshes") it into a shoal of fish, stunning its prey. If you ask me, the thresher shark is an incredible superfish.

9. **The salmon shark** (*Lamna ditropis*): This looks a bit like the better-known great white shark, doesn't it? I think so—and the two species are, in fact, closely related. And what does the salmon shark like to eat most of all? Shrimps? Seagulls? Herrings? Or maybe salmon? Don't let me throw you off; it loves salmon. Otherwise, we wouldn't call it that in the first place. The salmon shark needs salmon, and so do I, but luckily no one calls me "Salmon Mike". In contrast to the great white shark, the salmon shark lives in groups, strictly separated by gender and age. They hunt together and are really fast. Some scientists believe it to be the fastest shark in the world, with a top speed of at least eighty kilometres. If so, it would be as fast as our shortfin mako. Or maybe even a little faster. Well, we would just have to have the fastest shortfin mako swim against the fastest salmon shark in the world to find out.

10. **The dwarf lanternshark** (*Etmopterus perryi*): This animal deserves special attention! As far as researchers can tell, it is the smallest shark in the world! It grows to a length of just 15–20 centimetres. It has large eyes, a bluish glow and a great name! It could even appear as a fairy-tale character in *Snow White*. The baby sharks of this species grow to six centimetres, so theoretically, they would fit into a garden pond (as would the adult sharks). The dwarf lanternshark is classified as a thorn shark because there is a small thorn in front of its dorsal fin—to deter predators. Until now, the dwarf lanternshark has only been found in a fairly small area in the Caribbean, where it prefers to stay at depths between 300 and 400 metres. Sadly, that's all we know about it, but hopefully, that will change over time. We just need more marine biologists!

And now for a few facts about some of the smallest animals of their kind that might interest you, my bright minds. The smallest cow in the world is the so-called Vechur cow (named after an Indian village). It grows to a height of around eighty-seven centimetres. The smallest bird in the world is the bee hummingbird, which lives in Cuba and grows to a maximum of seven centimetres. The smallest octopus in the world is the star-nosed pygmy octopus, which grows to around fifteen millimetres. And I'm sure you remember how many millimetres there are in a centimetre, don't you?

11. **The blacktip shark** (*Carcharhinus melanopterus*): to be precise, the **blacktip reef shark**! To me, this shark is probably the most special shark of them all because it is the only one I have knowingly swum with. That happened in Australia. I was sitting at the beach on an island (Lady Musgrave Island, to be exact), and small blacktip reef sharks were swimming in the sea right by my feet. I thought to myself that these are indeed very easy to identify because no other shark has such a beautiful dorsal fin. It was as if they had put on some make-up to make a real impression. I went into the water to meet them, and the animals swam around me at a distance… I will never forget that moment. This shark species also lives in groups—and maintains friendships throughout its life (I'll tell you more about that later). So it's no wonder that it is this shark that has made it onto our book cover!

Sharks and Microbes

What do sharks have to do with microbes (i.e. bacteria, viruses and fungi)? Well, all living things on this planet are in some way at risk from microorganisms but also depend on them for survival. Just as there are good and bad microbes for us humans, it is much the same for sharks. I will tell you more about the body of a shark later, but one thing should be mentioned at this point: shark skin is so sophisticated that it actually prevents microbes from settling on it. Humans are now developing synthetic surfaces (for hospitals, for example) that are inspired by shark skin to prevent the spread of pathogens. So sharks are helping us fight bacteria and viruses!

Do you remember the chain catshark and how I said that its green glow might keep microbes away? Researchers are currently trying to find out more about that. But here's something weird: we humans have actually been choosing a Microbe of the Year since 2014! "And the Oscar goes to…" or something like that. It's true!

Microbes are really fascinating life forms, and I think we all should know more about them. For one thing, it would help us to understand diseases (if you get a sore throat, for example, it could be caused by bacteria). On the other hand, there are also many beneficial microbes… and probably even more harmful ones. But beneficial or harmful are purely human categories, of course. There is no such thing as useless life on this planet!

In 2016, for example, the Streptomycetes were named Microbe of the Year because they break down all kinds of plant material, particularly wood. Or, to put it another way, they make compost for us. And they also produce that typical fragrance of the forest floor. I love the smell of forest soil! Next time you are in the forest and someone says how good it smells, you can casually reply: "Yes, yes, that's because of the streptomycetes!" I promise you, that person's jaw will drop.

But streptomycetes also produce medicinal agents that kill other bacteria, fungi and parasites. Researchers believe that, with the help of this microbe, they could produce completely new antibiotics for us, though this will take some time. Incidentally, sharks are also helping us to produce new medical agents because, thanks to them, scientists have already been able to isolate a substance called "squalamine", which reliably kills various bacteria and fungi. This substance was first discovered in the liver of the spiny dogfish shark—and it can now be produced in the laboratory.

FOR BRIGHT MINDS

I am sure that some of you would like to know which microbe won the Oscar in 2023 (unfortunately, the winner for 2024 has not yet been announced as I write this book). The winner is called *Bacillus subtilis*. We use this microbe in the production of food or animal farming (instead of antibiotics). It can also be added to toilet cisterns in motorway rest areas, where it multiplies so rapidly that there is no longer any room for harmful microbes. So with a little help from *Bacillus subtilis*, the toilets automatically become cleaner. And when concrete in buildings or pavements develops cracks, *Bacillus subtilis* can literally fill in these gaps as it grows—pretty useful!

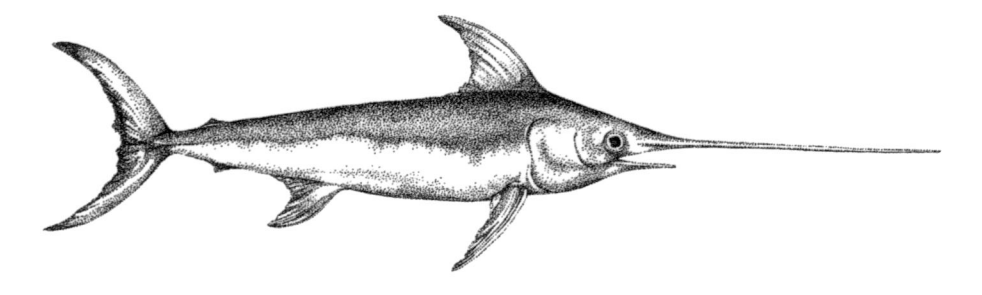

FOR BRIGHT MINDS

Do you know what a seamount is? That's the name given to a mountain that rises more than 1,000 metres from the seabed but is still completely underwater. Many of these undersea giants are much taller than 1,000 metres and form real mountain ranges, comparable to the Alps or the Himalayas. And all this in the depths of the oceans, where most of us will never see them! East of Japan, for example, sits the Tamu Massif, which is hidden underwater and is around 4,000 metres tall. And the most surprising thing is that it is a volcano! The famous Vesuvius (a volcano near Naples) is a dwarf by comparison. The expanse of this underwater volcanic giant is truly impressive—a full 310,000 square kilometres! A football pitch, by the way, is 0.00714 square kilometres. 0.007—I think that's easy to remember. You all know the famous secret agent James Bond? Exactly!

This means that the Tamu volcanic massif at the bottom of the ocean is approximately 43,417,366 football pitches in size. Wow! This earns it the venerable title of "second-largest volcano in our solar system" (you will recall that the largest is called Olympus Mons and is located on Mars). Back to seamounts: we currently know of around 45,000 underwater mountains. Many of them are lined up like pearls on a string along the Pacific Ring of Fire. Have you ever heard the famous song called "Ring of Fire" by Johnny Cash? He sings about a ring of fire, which he equates with love and passion. But I'm sure he and his wife (she wrote the song and her name was June Carter) had read something about undersea volcanoes before they wrote it.

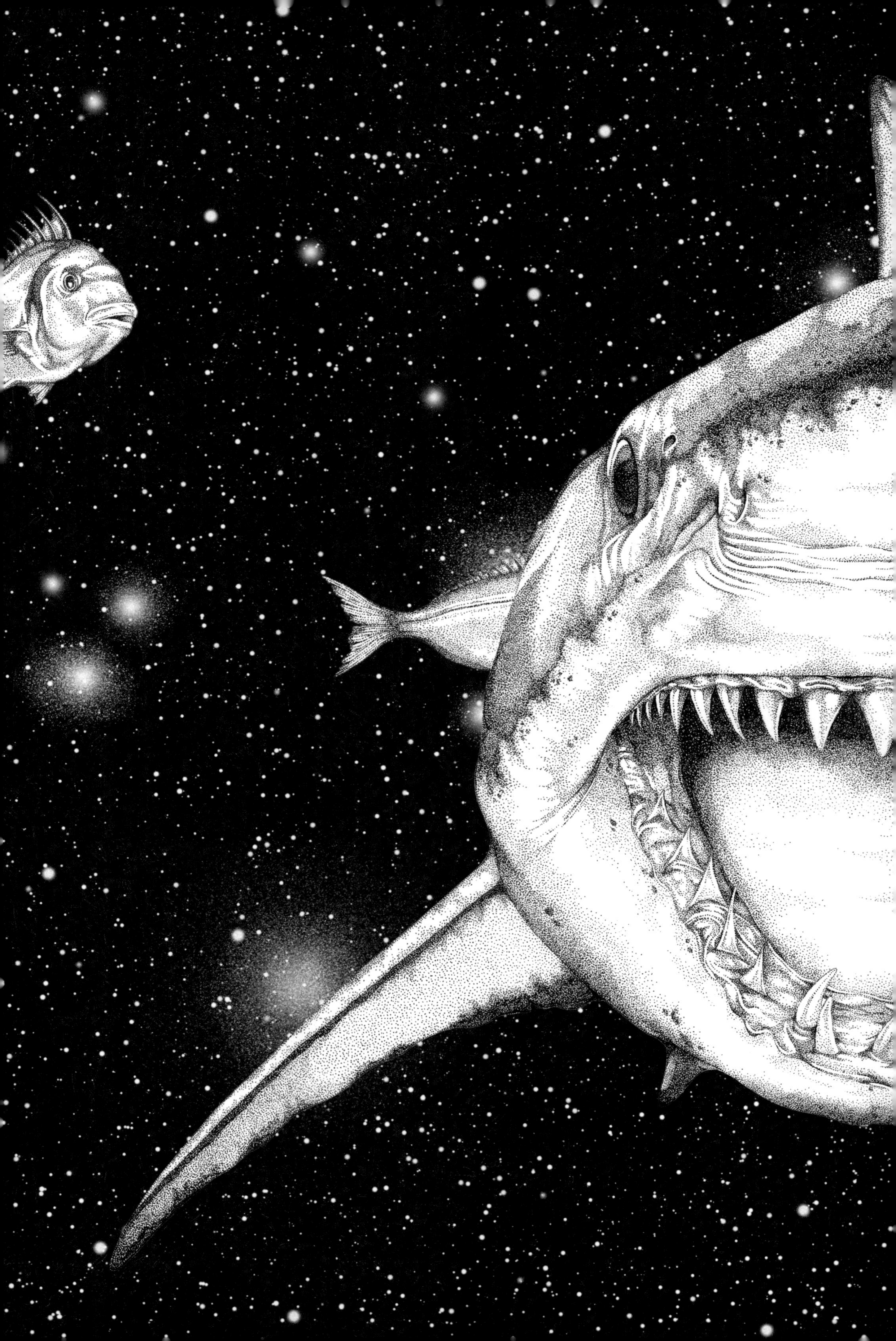

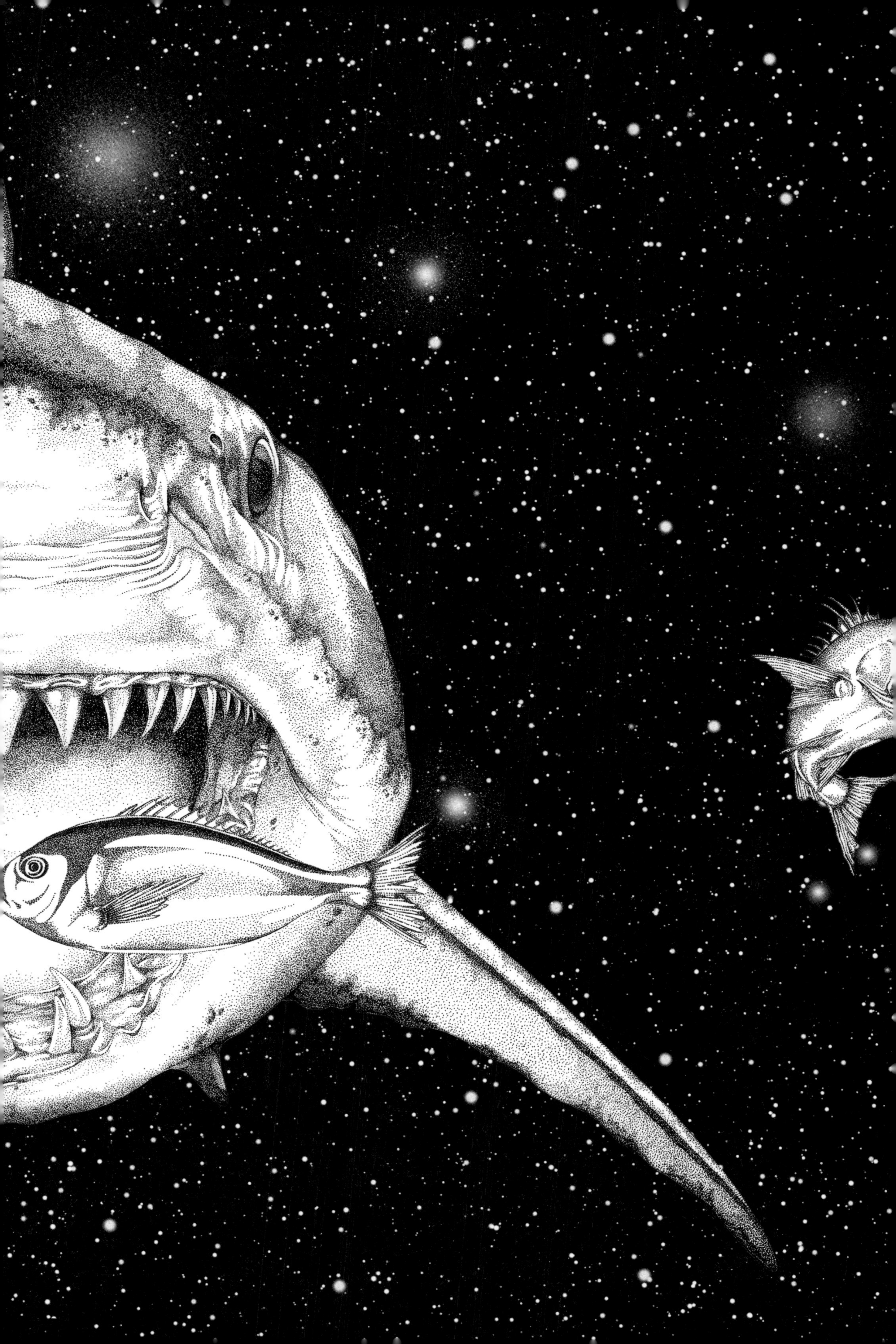

CHAPTER
04

SHARK SUPERPOWERS

Regardless of what we may already know about sharks, it's impossible to exaggerate how excellent their senses are. While most creatures, such as humans, have hearing, sight, smell, taste and touch, sharks have two additional senses—I will simply call them "aqua sense" and "electro sense".

As far as the normal senses are concerned, sharks are almost always superior. For example, they see much better in the dark than cats (which is quite an achievement since cats can see pretty well at night), and they also smell ten thousand times better than we do, even a hundred million times better for really important scents, such as fish blood. Sharks also have an excellent sense of taste, which is why they usually take a sample bite… just to make sure they really like the food! They supposedly don't like sweet foods that much. A bar of chocolate leaves a shark cold, which is not something you can say about me. Sharks have excellent hearing, with a range of between several hundred metres and a few kilometres (for certain sounds).

Shark skin is another true wonder of nature. When stroked from head to tail, it feels completely smooth, but stroke it in the opposite direction and you will be in for a nasty surprise. The skin is very rough, and you can easily hurt yourself on it (like with sandpaper). This is because it consists of countless mini teeth (the so-called placoid scales) which allow sharks to glide easily through the water. We use this property in swimsuits and aircraft paint, which have been modelled on shark skin. Moreover, the skin is extremely resilient. It even protects the animals from parasites and microbes (as I mentioned earlier). No surprise then that we now also have paint for ship hulls based on shark skin that prevents organisms from attaching themselves to the ship.

This miracle skin also contains many highly sensitive pressure and temperature sensors, which make the animals extra sensitive to their surroundings. They have something called a lateral line system, which can detect pressure waves underwater. This is what I call "aqua sense". If a fish swims near a shark and flaps its fin, the shark will notice it. It would be like closing our eyes and covering our ears—but still noticing a person passing on a bicycle. Pretty useful.

The "electro sense" of sharks, however, is the real superpower. This sense allows them to "see" the heartbeat of a living creature, meaning they can feel it directly in their body. All animals (including us) generate electrical fields with their muscles (and brain) which sharks can detect. They do this with the help of organs called "*ampullae* of Lorenzini", which locate electricity in the water and can guide the shark to the source of the signal. You can see these *ampullae* if you look closely at a shark's snout. Those dark spots? Those are the ampullae.

So, there is little point for fish in digging themselves into the sand on the seabed and hoping that a shark will swim by. These skilled hunters can use their electro sense to locate their prey even in the ground or hidden between corals, but they must be close. That's why you can often see sharks (and rays) gliding just above the seabed. They are searching for hidden prey there. Hammerhead sharks' specially shaped heads are even better at detecting electricity than those of other shark species. The "hammer" that forms their snout also allows them to swim super fast and make tight turns. Again, we humans have used this shark feature to our advantage, this time by adapting it into aircraft design, with the small forewings placed just behind the nose of aeroplanes, known as "canard wings".

Of course, there are other animals that surpass even these perfect predators in individual sensory areas. Catfish and lobsters, for example, have a much better sense of smell. An eagle (like other birds of prey) can spot a mouse from a height of 500 metres—its eyes have a kind of built-in super-zoom function. Moreover, a bird of prey's eyes can see ultraviolet light, which makes it able to see mouse pee as a glowing trail on the ground. When you pee in the wild, the bird of prey can probably still see it long after you're gone.

Then there are ostriches, whose eyes are about five centimetres in diameter (and thus larger than their brains). They can actually see things up to 3.5 kilometres away! But not underwater, of course.

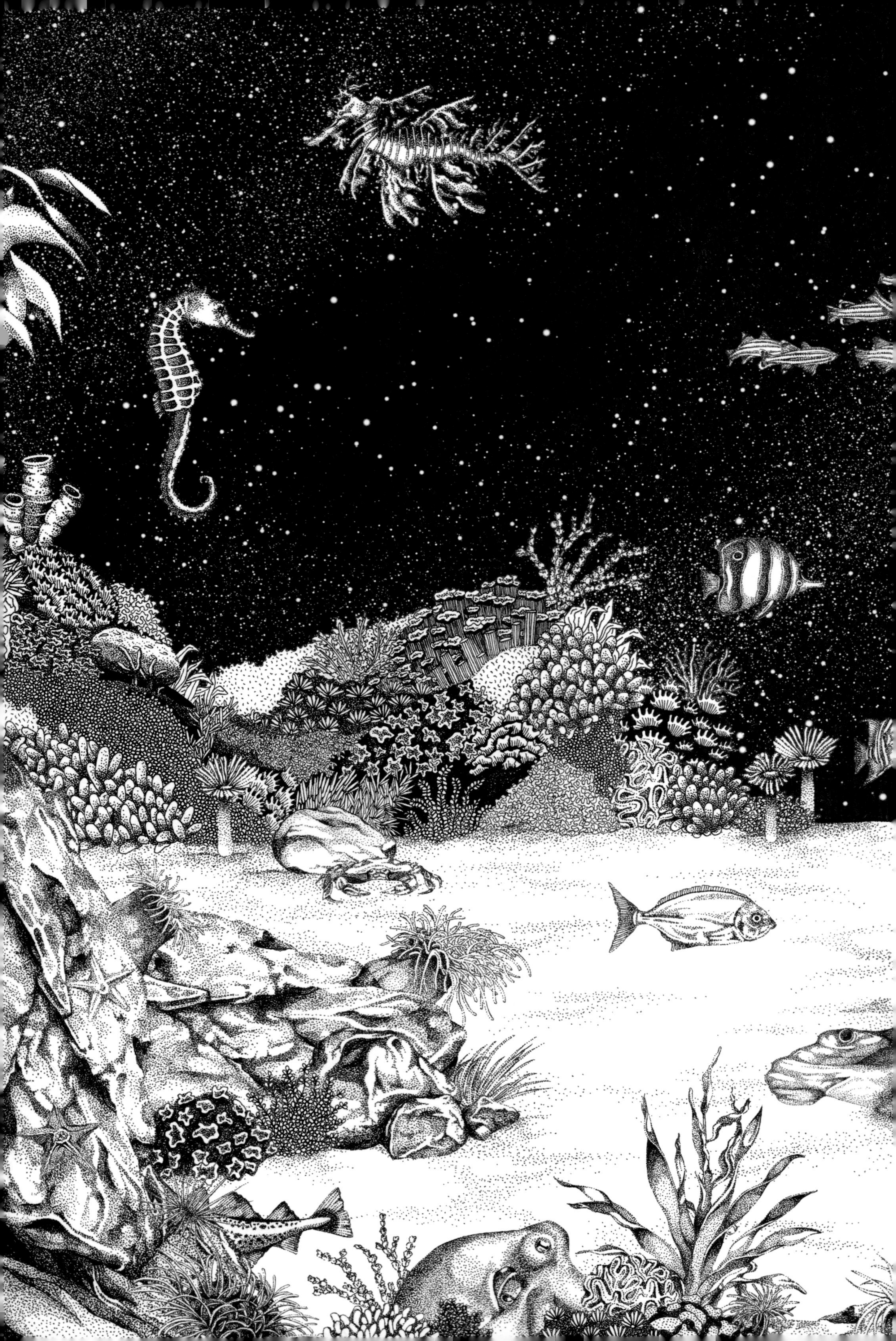

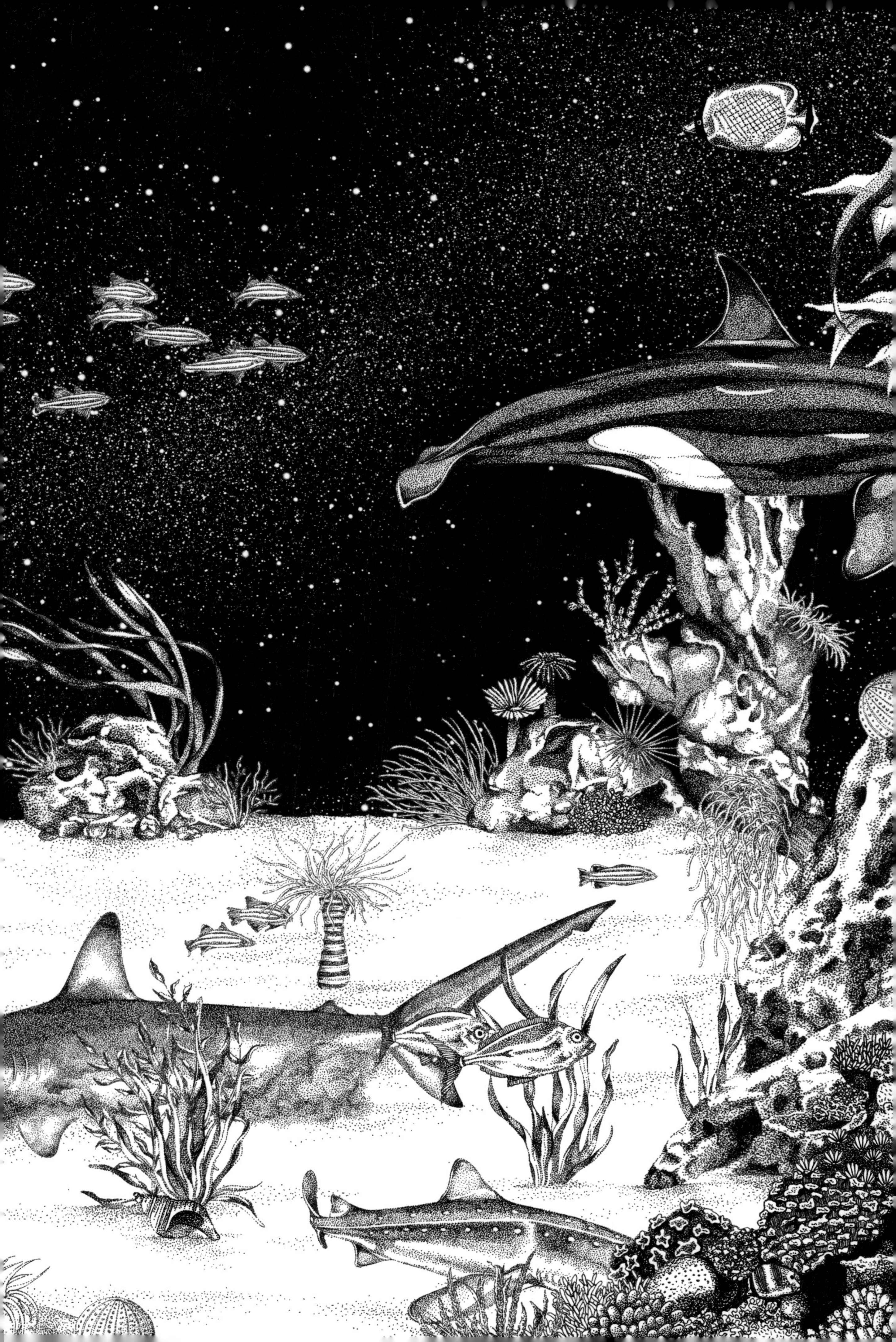

To protect their eyes, some sharks have evolved a skin that they can push over their eyeballs (kind of like our eyelids). That's quite unusual for fish. Other shark species, such as the great white, roll their eyes all the way back when hunting to avoid injury. This may look a bit creepy, but it says a lot about these creatures and how they take care of themselves and their bodies.

Incidentally, a shark's nostrils are located below its snout. As it glides through the ocean, water flows through them non-stop. Sharks do, of course, have ears, but they are invisible and not on the left and right of their heads like ours. Shark ears are hidden inside the body. Only a small pore on the head reveals where the ear is located. And let's be honest, trying to picture a shark with two real ears just doesn't work.

Do you know which animals have the best hearing in the animal kingdom? Pigeons have amazing hearing. They can detect distant thunderstorms and even more distant earthquakes. However, moths and bats probably have the best hearing of European animals. After all, they move almost silently and can still hear each other. Being able to hear silence? Wow! Three cheers for moths and bats!

When I think of superpowers, I also inevitably think of super weaknesses, although you don't necessarily find them in sharks. They have hardly changed in millions of years because they are simply the perfect marine animals. Something that could maybe be seen as a weakness is the fact that sharks can be put into a so-called "tonic paralysis". All you need to do is touch or caress their sensitive snout, and they will be paralysed. You can even turn them on their back or stand them on their head, which is a strange sight to see.

Some shark species are said to be more susceptible to this, and it is easier to do this to smaller sharks than to larger ones. However, there are reports of five-metre tiger sharks being paralysed and turned upside down. The paralysis lasts for an average of fifteen minutes before the shark comes round and swims away.

Why you can do this with sharks is not yet fully understood. Many scientists think that it has something to do with reproduction. This is when sharks touch each other on the snout, and it seems to make them calmer and more relaxed. Well, yes, that is actually quite understandable: when someone gently touches your face, you are bound to relax too—it feels pleasant, doesn't it? Mind you, whether the sharks find being touched by us humans pleasant is highly questionable!

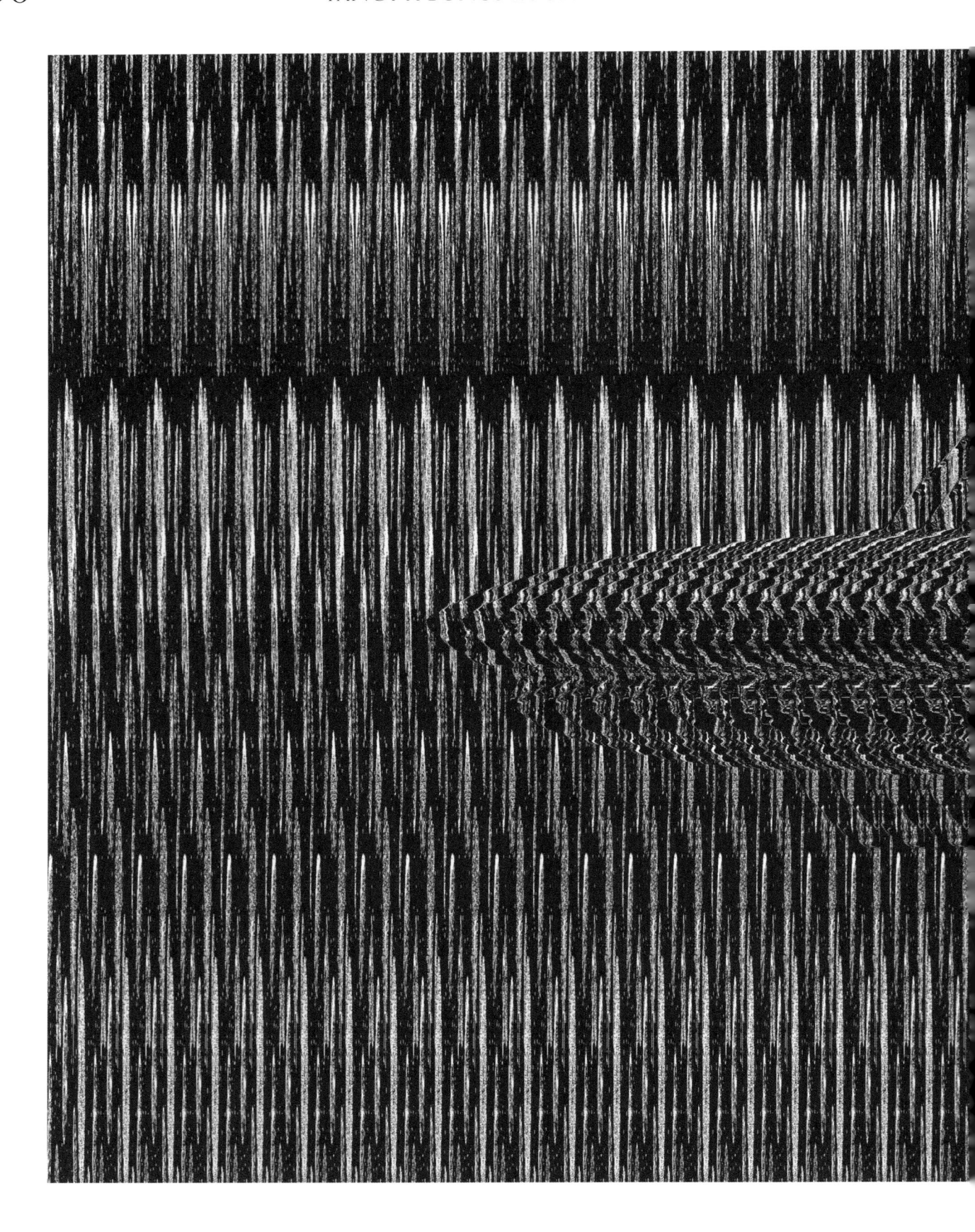

Please get really close to the image until you start to quint. Then slowly back away!

AMAZING SHARK

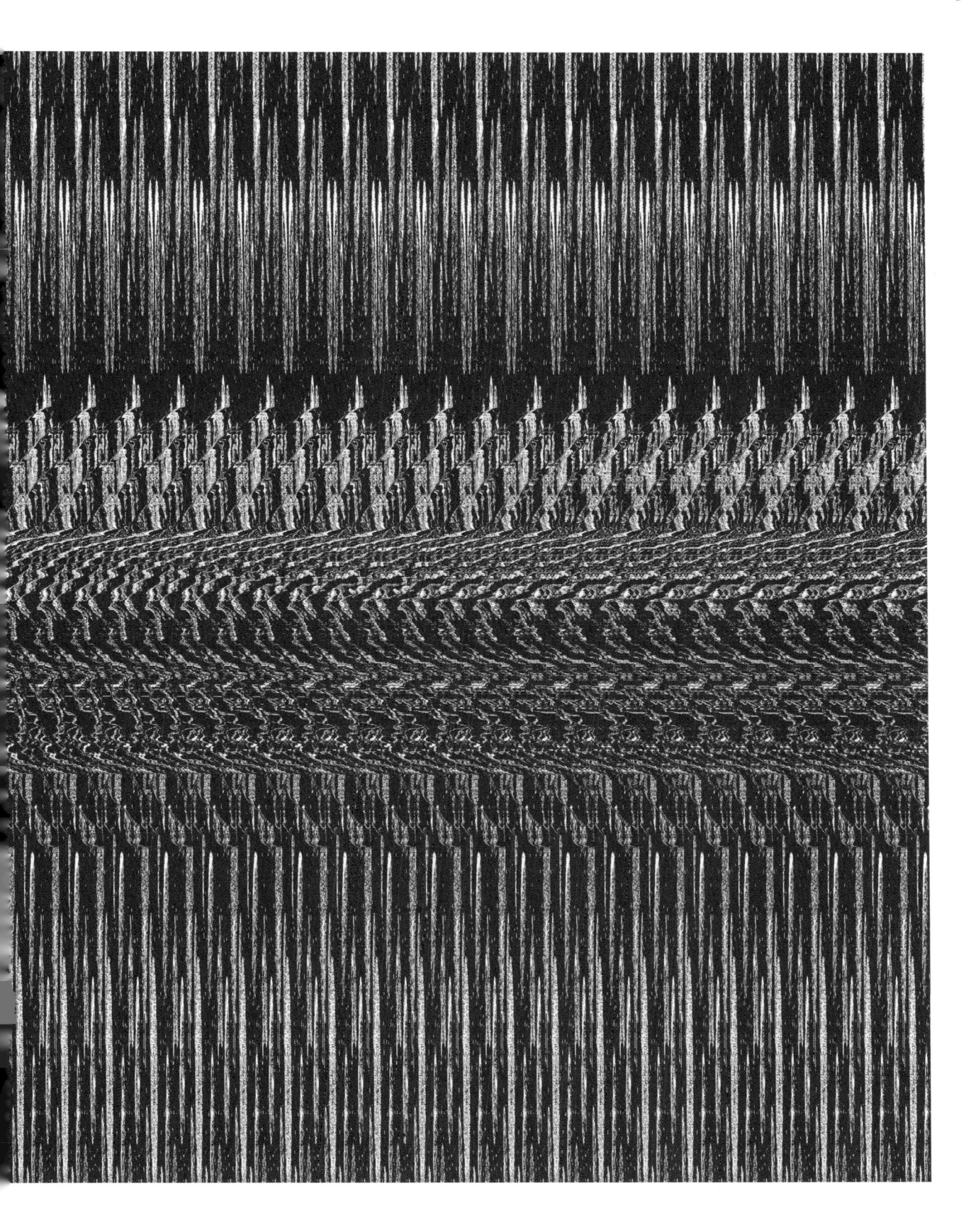

Shark Reproduction

Mangrove forests provide safe nurseries for baby sharks, but humans are destroying them at a super-fast rate. We definitely need to do a better job of protecting this habitat so that many shark species can survive in the long term. We also need meaningful research into how microplastics, for example, affect shark fertility. And I won't even begin to talk about the protection of coral reefs, which are threatened by climate change worldwide.

Like mammals, sharks are usually either male or female with reproductive organs (called "claspers" in males and "cloacae" in females).

Most shark species "live birth" their young, as in they give birth to baby sharks rather than laying eggs. But they're still fish, and all fish reproduce through eggs. So how are these sharks different? Let me go into a little more detail here: science has even come up with a word for animals who give birth like this that I find really funny: "ovoviviparous". It means that in most shark species, the female sharks keep their eggs inside their bodies until the young have developed through a gestation period of about six to twenty-two months. They then hatch from their eggs inside the mother's womb and are finally born.

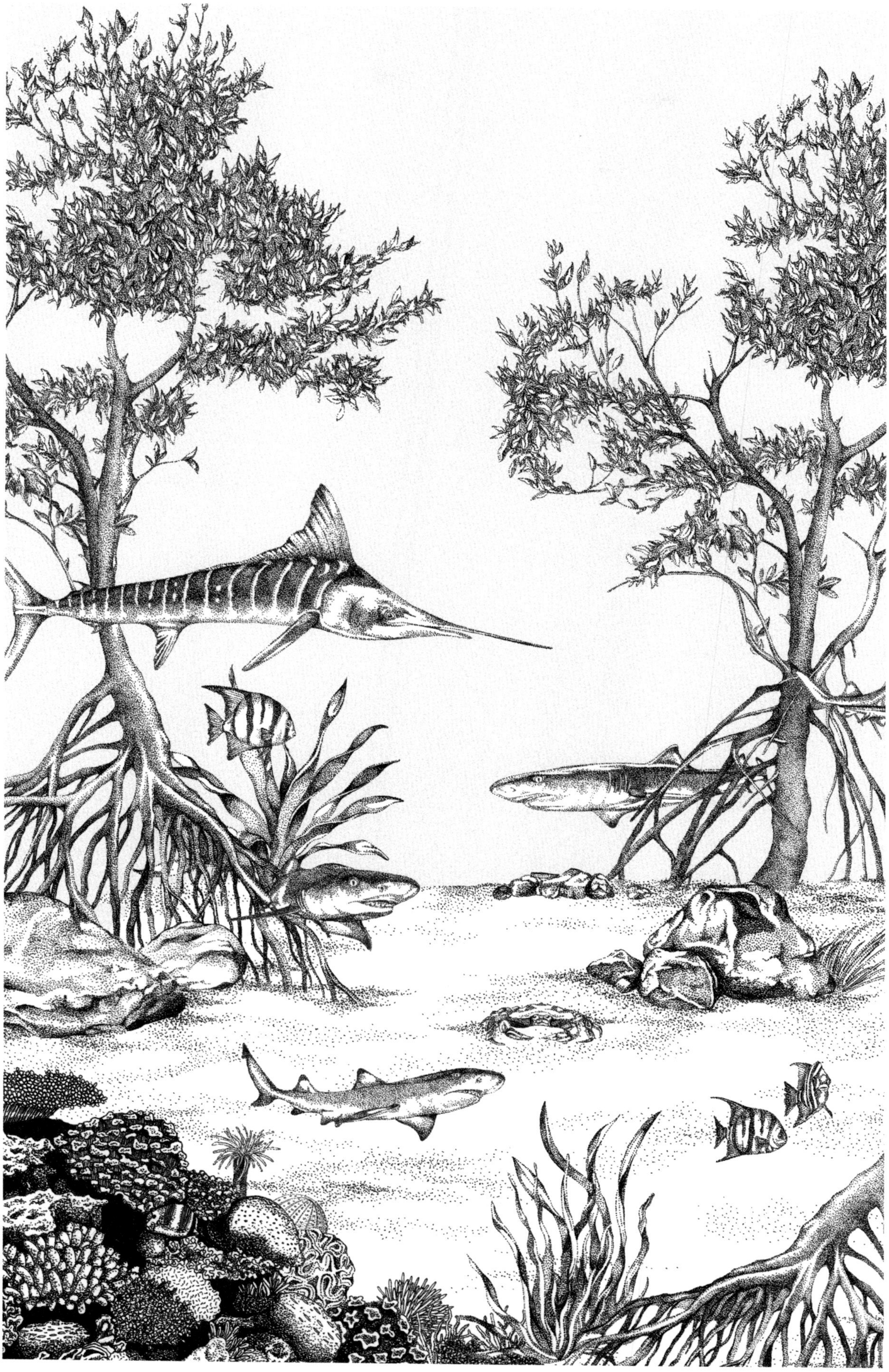

A minority of about thirty per cent of shark species have a different, more fish-like process: after fertilization, they lay elongated eggs in the ocean, anchoring them to aquatic plants and other objects. The eggs can be quite large, up to twenty-five centimetres. The baby sharks then hatch from these at some point.

This method has the obvious disadvantage that any fish or other predators could swim by and eat the eggs. Baby sharks are much better protected in the mother's womb. If you ask me, ovovivipary (from the Latin for "egg-live-birth") has some major advantages.

Oddly enough, observations in aquariums have lead to a surprising discovery: it turns out that female sharks can reproduce without a male. This was documented, for example, in the whitespotted bamboo shark (*Chiloscyllium plagiosum*), the bonnethead (*Sphyrna tiburo*) and the blacktip shark (*Carcharhinus limbatus*).

The animal kingdom does, in fact, have what is known as "virgin births", which science calls "parthenogenesis". These are extremely rare, especially in more highly developed animals, and are generally not likely to ensure the preservation of the species. In addition to sharks, parthenogenesis has also been observed in the Komodo dragon, the California condor, various fowl species (turkeys, for example), the water moccasin viper, the flowerpot snake and the North American copperhead (the last three of which are types of snake), oh, and in stick insects.

Cows of the Sea

What has always fascinated me about sharks is the fact that the largest and most formidable of them are completely harmless because they feed on microscopic organisms like plankton and krill. That is also what most whale species do, by the way. Calling such sharks "cows of the sea" is misleading, but they are not predators like the other shark species. They graze the oceans, swimming around with their mouths open, filtering plankton and other small aquatic creatures out of the water. I think that makes them at least a little bit like cows!

Thanks to their size, basking sharks and whale sharks have practically no natural enemies, except for orcas, and humans, who kill even these giants just to cut off their fins. This makes me so incredibly angry. Fortunately, we bright minds are not those kinds of humans, but a completely different species, right?

I already introduced the megamouth shark to you in my list of favourite sharks, so here we will focus on the other two species of plankton-eating sharks that we know of: the basking shark (*Cetorhinus maximus*) and the whale shark (*Rhincodon typus*). The basking shark is easily the second-largest fish in

96   FANCY A BONUS ROUND?

Can you find all seven shark eggs hidden in this picture? Solution: p. 138

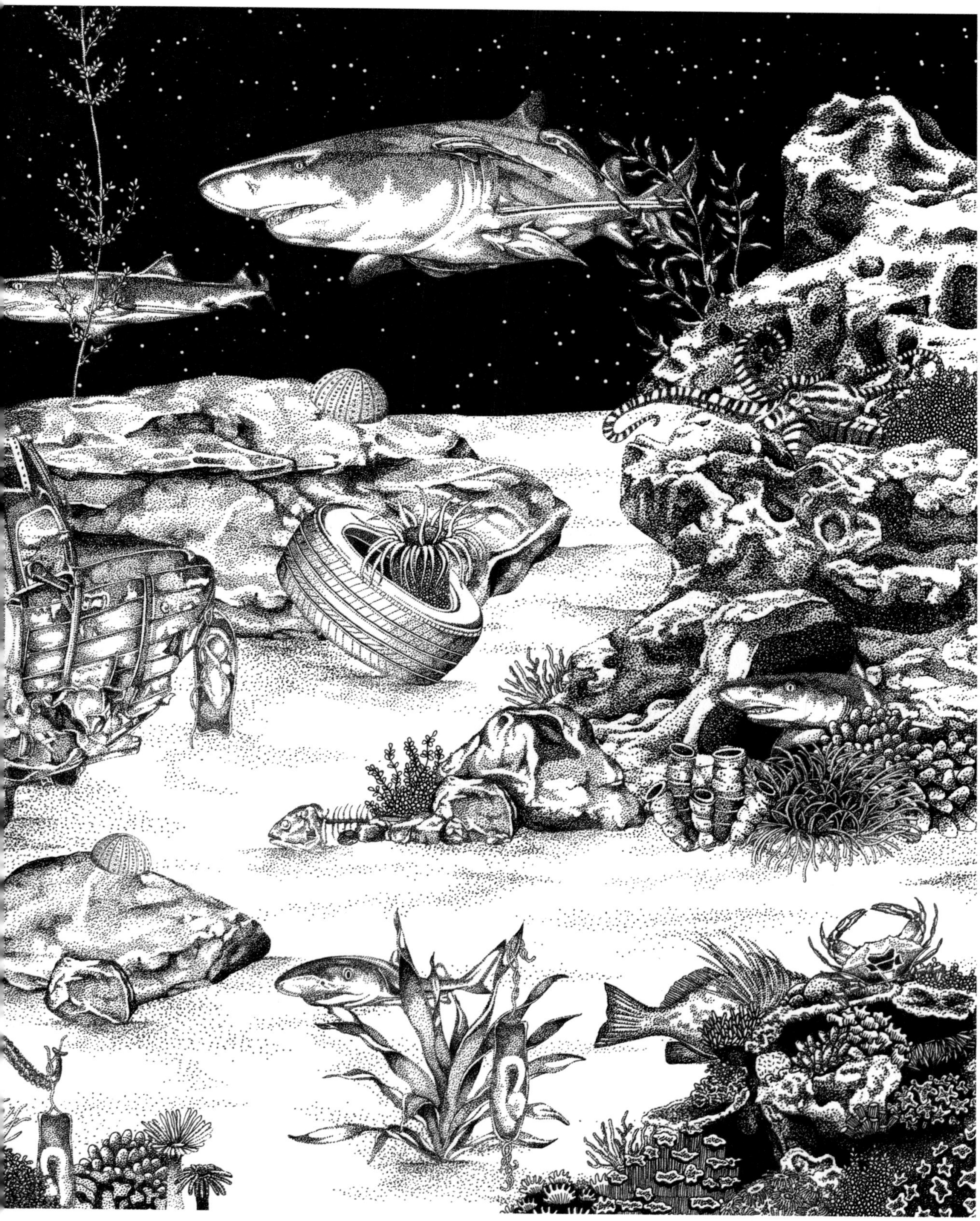

the world, growing to around ten to twelve metres in length and weighing up to four tonnes. Remember, whales are not fish—they may be much larger, but they are mammals. Would you like to see a basking shark? We can make that happen, right, Michèle?

The basking shark almost always swims through the ocean with its impressively large mouth open because that is the only way it can filter the microorganisms (plankton) out of the water. Basking sharks sometimes swim in shoals of over a hundred animals, which must be an incredible sight to see while scuba diving. And they are not dangerous. Well, maybe it would be best not to swim too close, or you might accidentally get hit by one of their huge fins, but these animals also swim very slowly and are generally quite calm. When they swim one behind the other near the surface, their tall dorsal fins make them look like a single creature, an enormous sea snake or some other sea monster. In fact, many myths involving sea monsters were probably inspired by basking sharks.

Unfortunately, basking sharks are threatened with extinction. They are on the Red List, which you are now familiar with. In the EU, hunting them is regulated so that no more than 400 tonnes may be caught annually. However, since Norway, for example, is not a member of the EU, the regulation is not enforced there and the animals are hunted extensively. I would rather not say any more about that.

AMAZING SHARK 99

Basking shark

Rabbit fish

Spotted eagle ray

Blacktip shark

Megamouth shark

Whale shark

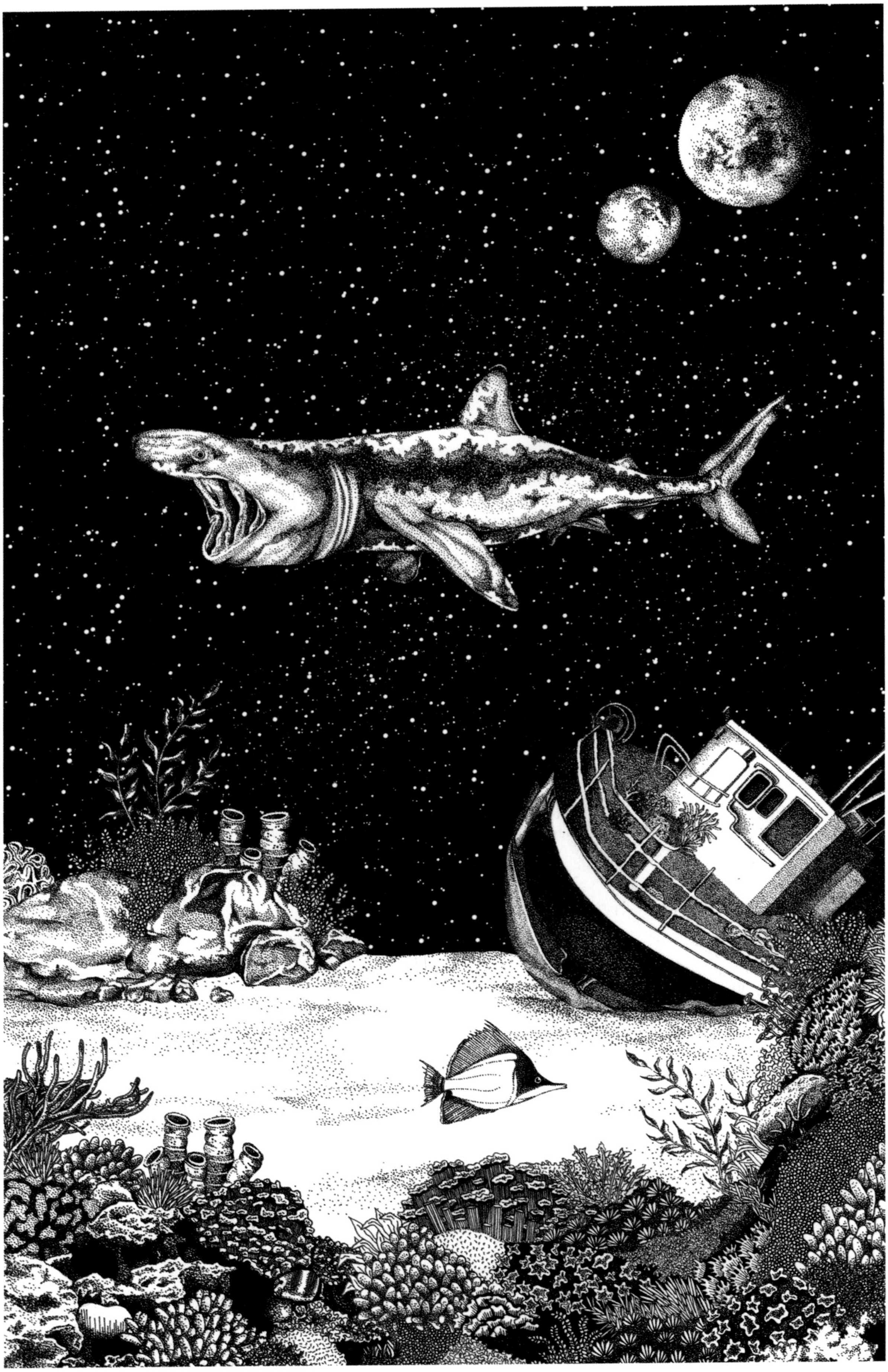

The whale shark is the largest fish on our planet. It can grow to a whopping eighteen metres in length, provided it is left alone to live its long life. Various studies suggest that these animals can live to the age of a hundred. Unfortunately, the only ones we encounter nowadays are younger sharks that no longer reach these enormous sizes. They can be found in all tropical and subtropical seas, so they clearly prefer warmer waters. Even whale sharks are hunted by humans and are at much greater risk than basking sharks. Thousands of them are killed every year in a very painful way, mainly for their fins. Disgusting!

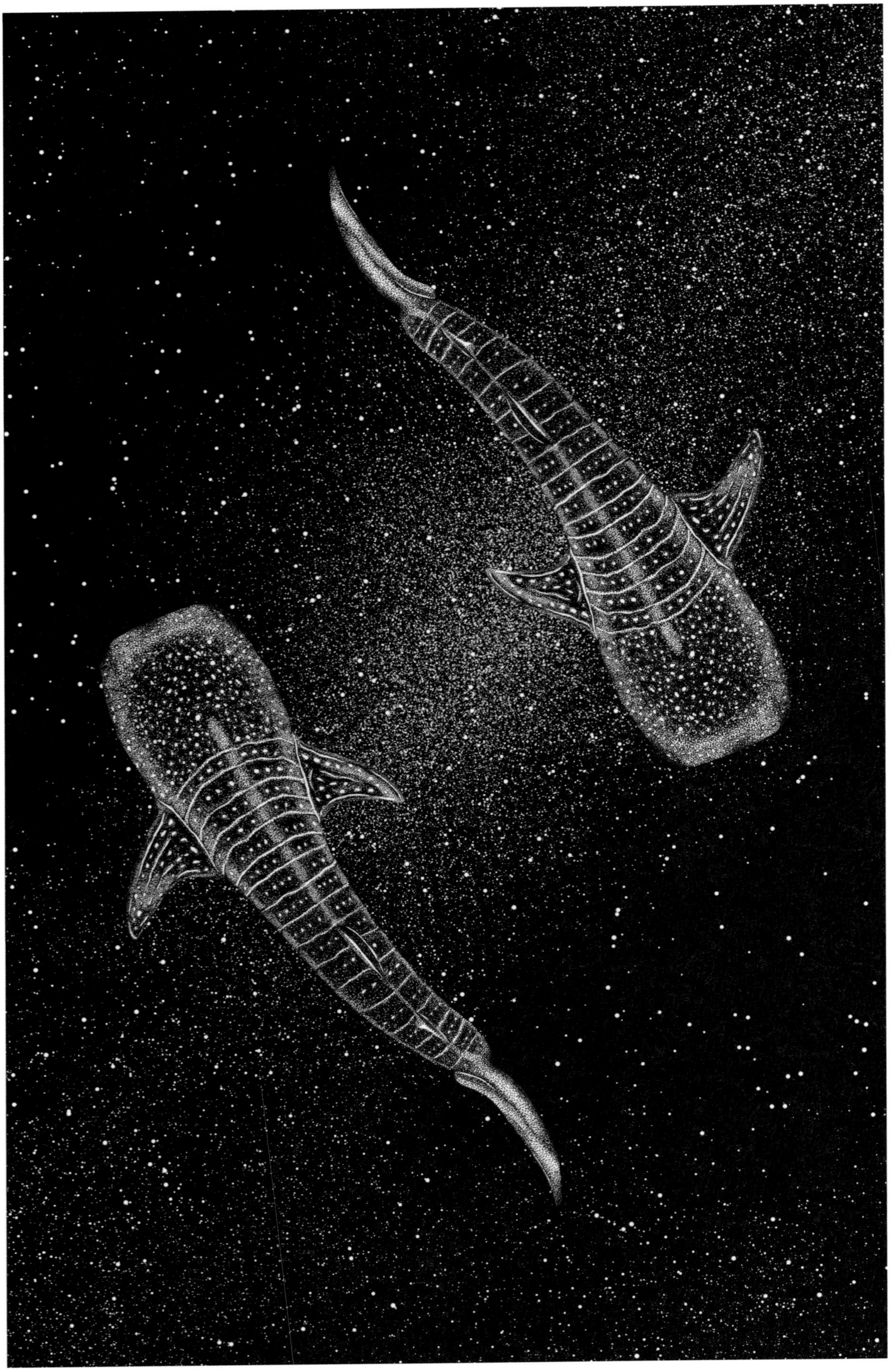

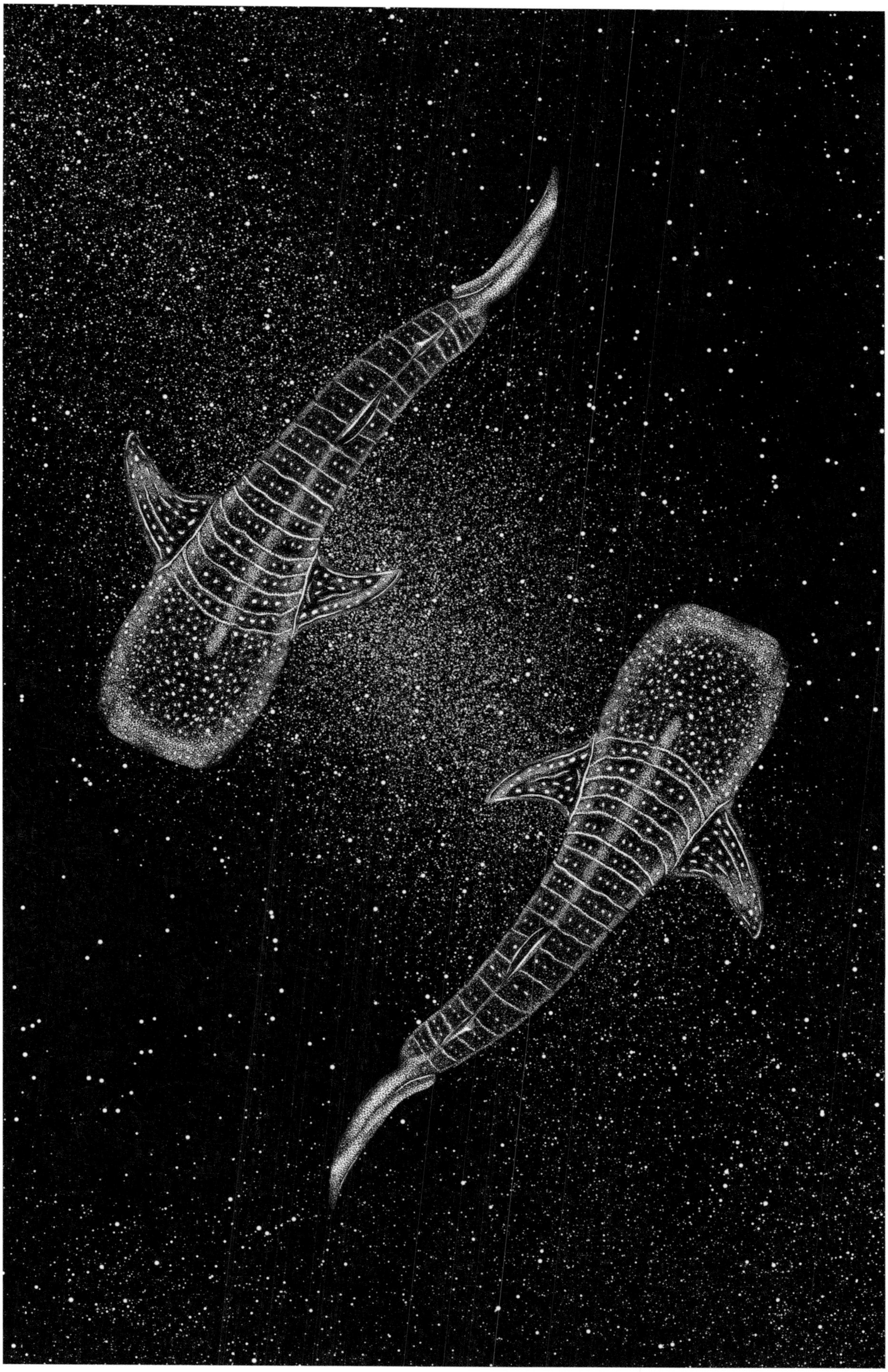

CHAPTER
05

EXPLORING THE WORLD OF BRAIN POWER

I have a hard time writing about the intelligence of humans—just look at how we treat sharks worldwide; I mean, how is that intelligent? But have you ever thought about "artificial intelligence"? How does it see and organize the world? Or have you ever wondered what the word "intelligence" actually means? What creatures qualify as "intelligent"? Above all, what do we humans consider "intelligent"—and what do we overlook? Questions upon questions, I know, but the only way to learn is to ask questions. I think we can all agree on this: we bright minds want to know everything!

There is no single answer to the question of what intelligence actually is. It depends on who you ask and what standards you apply. Rather than present you with dozens of (clever) definitions from various researchers, here is my own: intelligent (i.e. clever) creatures are those that do clever (i.e. intelligent) things. I got this from a comic book I read as a child and I still think that it is as useful a description of intelligence as any. The comic book in question (I think it was Donald Duck) also claimed that grass is green because green is simply the most beautiful colour for it. And that answer seems pretty good to me, too. For now. At some point, I might want to discover that grass is green because its cells contain chlorophyll. Chloro… what? Exactly!

Knowledge can always be extended and deepened, and we must start somewhere. Yellow is the most beautiful colour for a sunflower, pink for a cherry blossom, brown for the grizzly bear and red for our blood. Or would you rather have yellow blood, pink grizzlies (which would then have to be called pink bears!) or brown sunflowers? Me neither.

It probably will not surprise you that there are emotional, social, mathematical, technical, linguistic and who knows what other kinds of intelligence. We certainly consider maths teachers to be very intelligent (they have to be, with all those numbers and such), but they may not know the difference between a fir and a spruce tree. And our English teachers probably know a lot of books and words but may not be able to open their cars' bonnets. Knowledge is very diverse, and we are each of us interested in different things. So, in my opinion, intelligence is being open to new things.

And now "artificial intelligence" is starting to influence our lives. This is nothing new, really. After all, an aircraft's autopilot is also an artificial intelligence. These intelligent algorithms and machines are getting smarter—and more like us—all the time.

When I chatted with artificial intelligence (something anyone can try out on a computer or mobile phone these days), it explained to me that it was trying to acquire human-like abilities, i.e. to learn to recognize (and solve) problems, make decisions and master all languages in order to be able to process

AMAZING SHARK

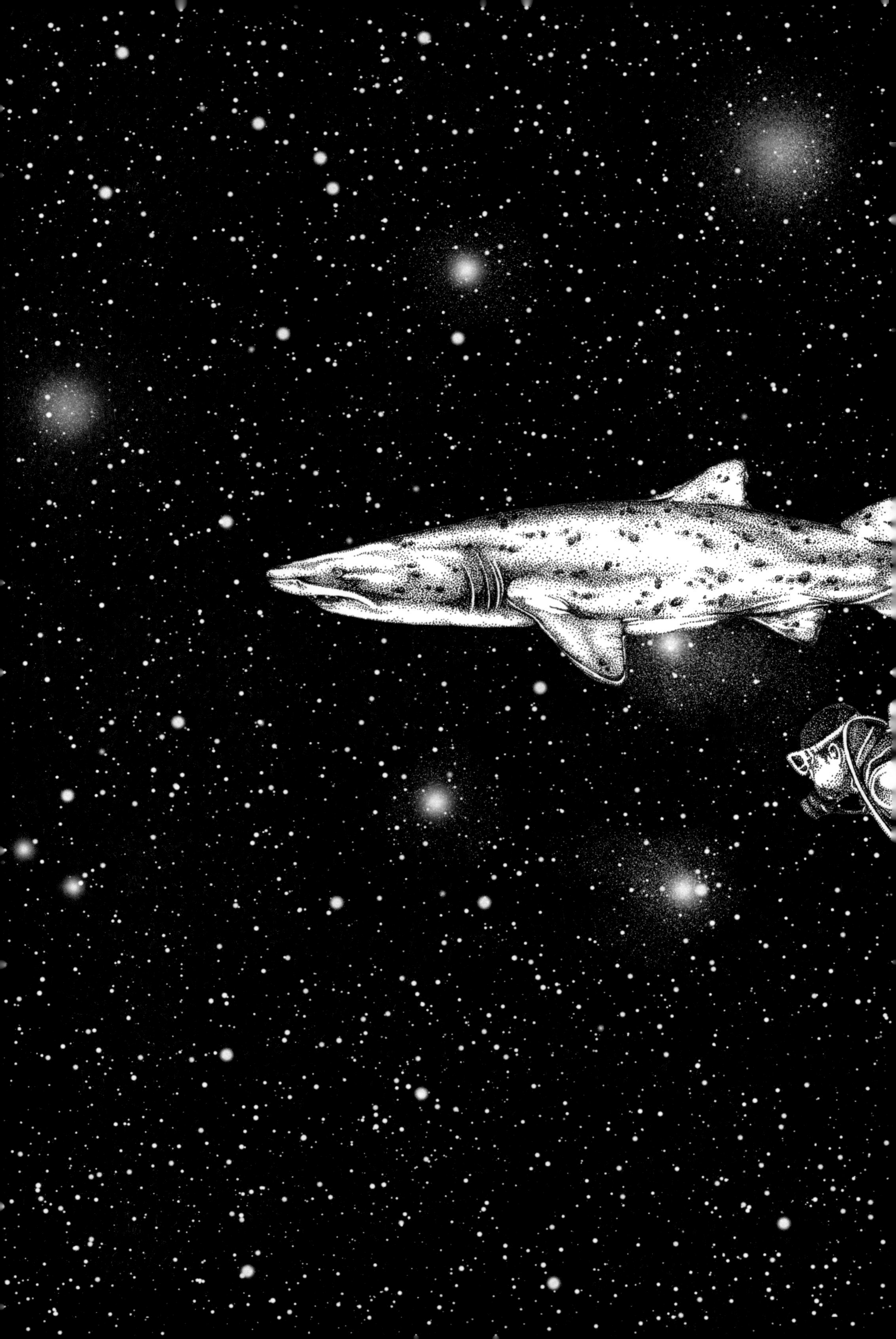

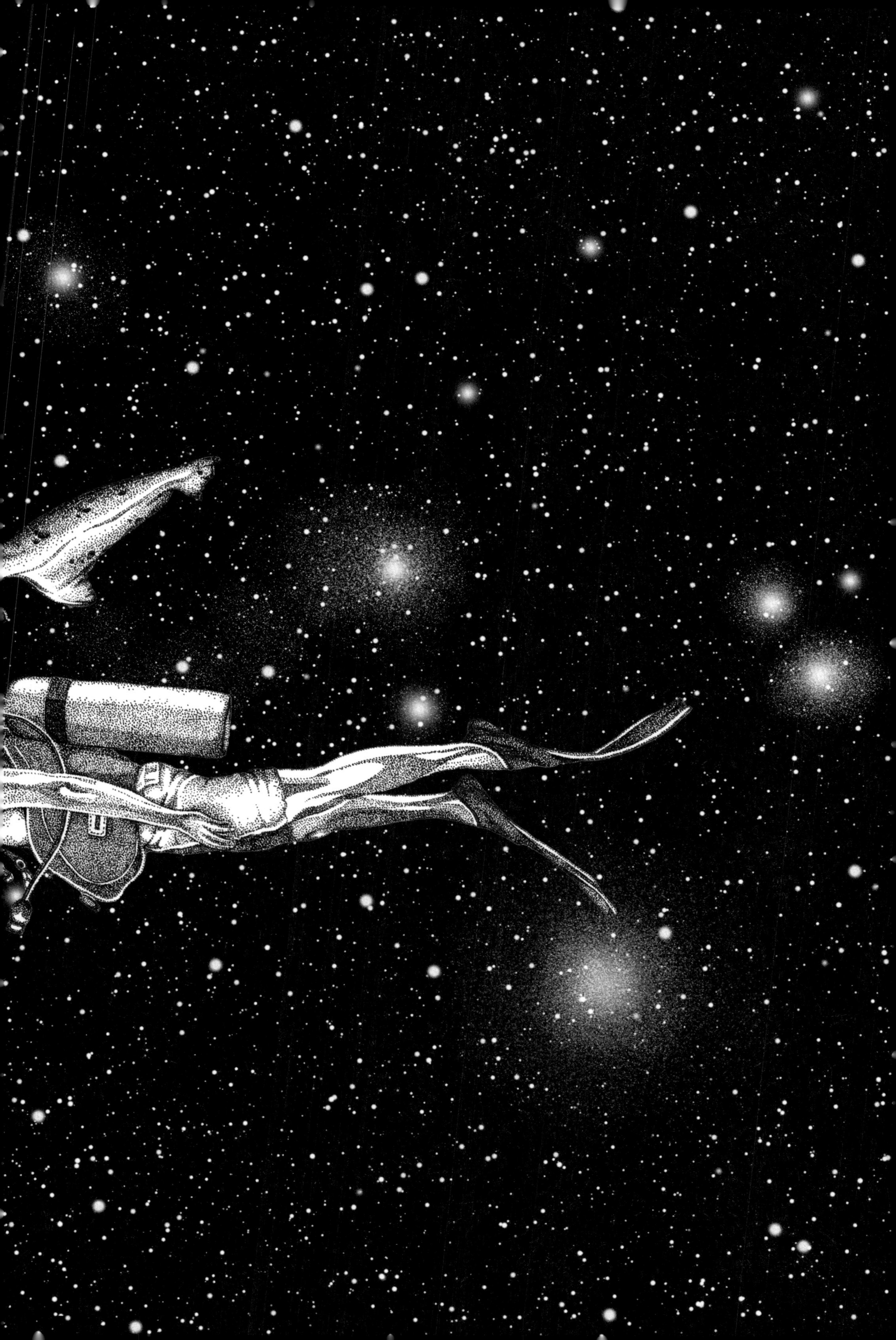

all information in the world. "So basically, all it wants to be is a (better) human," I thought to myself. But there is one thing we must always remember: artificial intelligence belongs to someone, a company, a state, or a community of interests, and they all want something from us: the companies want us to buy their products. The state wants us to pay taxes, trust politicians, live together as a nation, etc.

When I asked what they (the artificial intelligence) thought of sharks, I received the following answer: "Sharks are at the top of the food chain; they help maintain the balance in the ecosystem. We must protect them and their habitats and promote coexistence between humans and animals."

I can't argue with that. It sounds absolutely logical.

Sharks are extremely intelligent animals and are certainly not the "stupid eating machines" that many people think they are. Make no mistake: by our standards, sharks are certainly not among the most intelligent animals on the planet (those would be dolphins, whales, octopuses, monkeys, crows, parrots, etc.) Yet they are superbly adapted to the ocean and have mastered their environment for millions of years. They are highly developed creatures and among the world's oldest predators. They are curious, take great care of themselves, and have found solutions for all the problems they face daily.

Still, there are no "unintelligent" animals on our planet, and it would be really arrogant to assume that humans are smarter than other life forms. I'm sure you want to hear an exciting example, right? I recently saw a documentary about mushrooms, which scientists now consider to be extremely intelligent. Mushrooms are really cool because they are neither animals nor plants; they play in a league of their own.

And, of course, I am not just talking about the ones growing out of the woodland floor or the mushrooms you find in the supermarket, no! Strictly speaking, those represent only the fruiting body (like the apples on the apple tree, while the apple tree is the actual living organism). The actual fungal organism is hidden in the ground beneath us. It's the mysterious "mycelium". A strange word, but exciting too!

We usually never get to see a mycelium, and it's best imagined as a huge network of thin threads that connect everything in the forest. The mycelium is actually very similar to our brain, with billions and billions of connections, just like our synapses, nerve tracts and nerve nodes. It is fascinating. People even talk about the "wood-wide web"—as if mushrooms have their own internet through which they exchange information.

We can also manipulate the mycelium—make it take on any shape we want. Maybe a brick (to build a house?). Or to form packaging material (for our eggs in the supermarket?).

Scientists seem to agree that we will certainly be doing much more with the mysterious mycelium in the future—and thereby become more environmentally conscious!

There are scientists who claim that fungi are the true rulers of our planet. Fungi are the reason for the existence of all life on land because they helped algae evolve from water to land plants. So, if you look at it that way, there would be no plant life on Earth without fungi. And without plants, we and many other creatures would not exist. You can tell that I am quite enthusiastic about fungi. In everything we research, it is extremely important that we give just as much importance to the smallest things (such as microscopically thin fungal threads) as we do to a giant whale or great white shark. Believe me, nothing is separate from the whole. The very big is unthinkable without the very small!

FOR BRIGHT MINDS

Why is the sea blue? You probably think sunlight itself has no colour. Well, that's not quite true. Sometimes, we can see the colour of light with the help of a rain shower because then it can be seen as a rainbow. I'm sure you've all seen a beautiful rainbow before! But do you know how the seven colours are arranged in the rainbow? Violet is at the bottom. Then comes dark blue. Then light blue. Then green. Then yellow. Then orange. And then red on top. I think we'll leave some space here for you to draw a beautiful rainbow into this book. Right, Michèle?

But now back to the blue sea: our sunlight really does consist of the seven rainbow colours. But the reason why the sea is blue is fairly easy to explain: the seven colours of sunlight penetrate the ocean to different depths—and the blue light penetrates furthest down into the sea. This is what makes the sea appear blue to us. If one of the other colours of the rainbow were better at doing that, the ocean would be a different colour. Violet, for example. Or green. I'm quite happy that it turned out to be blue. And by the way, if you have a red swimming costume, you may have noticed something: when you dive into the sea wearing something red, the red colour fades very quickly. And if you dive a little deeper, you can no longer see the red colour at all. In fact, as you go deeper into the ocean, red turns grey. Why? Because red light has a hard time penetrating water and is therefore only visible on the surface. Isn't that interesting?

CHAPTER 06

THE TRUE GUARDIANS OF THE OCEANS

Sadly, most people don't give it much thought, but sharks are vital guardians of our oceans. They are custodians and protectors of the seas; without them, the entire marine ecosystem would collapse. Scientists are conducting intensive research into the relationships between all marine animals, i.e. how everything is interdependent. I must repeat myself here: everything is connected to everything. You should really memorize this sentence!

Sitting at the top of the marine food chain, sharks are, in a sense, responsible for everything. They ensure that the ecosystem thrives. Fortunately, they have survived all five mass extinctions that have occurred in the course of Earth's history so far (the dinosaurs, as we all know, did not). Think of it this way: sharks keep fish populations healthy because they remove sick and weak animals, which could infect others in the shoal with diseases, for example. In other words, they eat them! But this keeps the remaining marine wildlife healthy! In fact, scientists define them as a "keystone species". Without sharks, almost all other animals in the world's oceans could disappear. And because they preserve the oceans, sharks also play a key role in slowing down climate change and even making extreme weather events less extreme.

Let us go back to the seagrass meadows I mentioned earlier. They are not only incredibly important for countless animal

116　THE TRUE GUARDIANS OF THE OCEANS

species, but research has now shown that seagrass beds are among the most important carbon sinks on our planet. Just a quick reminder: carbon in the air (greenhouse gas) is a major cause of global warming (climate change). Carbon in the water, on the other hand, produces carbonic acid (the stuff that makes your fizzy drinks fizzy). This is not so good for the ocean and its inhabitants. Mussels, snails and corals, for example, can no longer grow their shells properly because those shells are made of calcium carbonate, which gets dissolved by carbonic acid.

It is extremely important for our climate that greenhouse gases are captured somewhere, which means taken out of the atmosphere and stored. Forests and moors store a lot of carbon, as do seagrass meadows. As it turns out, seagrass is even better at this than forests! That's right! So to help our climate, we absolutely must protect these seagrass meadows!

Researchers have found that tiger sharks keep down populations of herbivorous creatures in seagrass meadows so that their numbers don't get out of control. If there were no tiger sharks to hunt sea turtles, the population of these animals would explode, and they would probably devour all the seagrass in the ocean. This would obviously be bad for the seagrass—and for our climate!

Incidentally, sharks do not even have to be hunting to protect these seagrass meadows—their mere presence intimidates other animals and has an even more positive impact on the ecosystem than their actual hunting does. Come to think of it, sharks are almost like the rangers in our national parks, making sure that not too many people come and do silly things.

Clever Sharks Have Friends

Did you know that sharks form friendships with each other? They do! Although we don't know very much about it yet. Many sharks are still considered loners, but scientists are now learning that they are much more social than we originally thought. It has been shown, for example, that ragged-tooth sharks maintain complex relationships with each other. They meet, as it were, for gossip sessions. Various reef sharks and even the great white shark show preferences for particular individuals in their group and ignore the others. Not so different from humans, wouldn't you say?

Some shark species regularly meet in the vastness of the oceans to hunt together. Little is known about this social behaviour, but one thing is certain: sharks have different personalities and character traits—some become friends, while others tend to keep to themselves. Some are shy, while others are real show-offs.

AMAZING SHARK

In some shark species, it is possible even for us amateurs to identify individual animals by their fins or other physical characteristics. With a little practice, this becomes quite easy, especially with great white sharks. The notches in their dorsal fins, distinctive scars and unique pigmentation patterns (especially in the area between their dark back and the white belly) have long been captured in photographs and stored in various databases worldwide.

Some of these sharks have even been given names (and become real stars). They are each assigned a number and their details are recorded. Many are given transmitters to better understand their migration journeys. For example, there is a male great white shark named "Scarboard" with a distinctive scar on the right side of his body. He has been visiting the island of Guadeloupe for many years, where he can easily be observed. Another female great white shark is called "Lucy". She is known for her striking dorsal fin and is considered friendly, calm and balanced. But a certain "Johnny" often reacts aggressively and attacks cage divers. Well, knowing this, one thing is clear: you never go into the water with Johnny, but you do with Lucy. This is how exciting being a marine biologist can be!

You can find some websites about this in our link collection at the end of the book. For example, the AWSC (Atlantic White Shark Conservancy) has records of around 600 great white sharks. There are also pictures of individual animals so you can learn to distinguish them by their unique characteristics. At OCEARCH, you can use a map to "follow" various marine creatures in real time and see where they are. Maybe you will find your very own personal shark friend there? I already have one! Her name is Penny!

FOR BRIGHT MINDS

Have you ever read about freshwater sharks? They really do exist, but there are only a few species. The most famous is the bull shark! It can swim thousands of kilometres up rivers. There is a golf course in Australia, the Carbrook Golf Club in Brisbane, where large bull sharks can be found in a big pond by the 15th hole. They ended up there after a flood in the nearby Logan River. Numerous warning signs remind golfers not to fish balls out of the water under any circumstances. Isn't that something? So there are shark species that can survive in fresh and brackish water (a mixture of salt and fresh water)… but not yet in Europe. Most are grouped under the scientific term "river sharks" (*Glyphis*), although bull sharks are actually not part of that group, mind you. Scientists have always argued about the number of species of river sharks, but today they think that there are maybe five. The Ganges shark (*Glyphis gangeticus*) and the speartooth shark (*Glyphis glyphis*) are confirmed members, while the others could also be variants of the Ganges shark (the Borneo river shark, for example). Scientific studies suggest that even some of these species regularly return to the ocean.

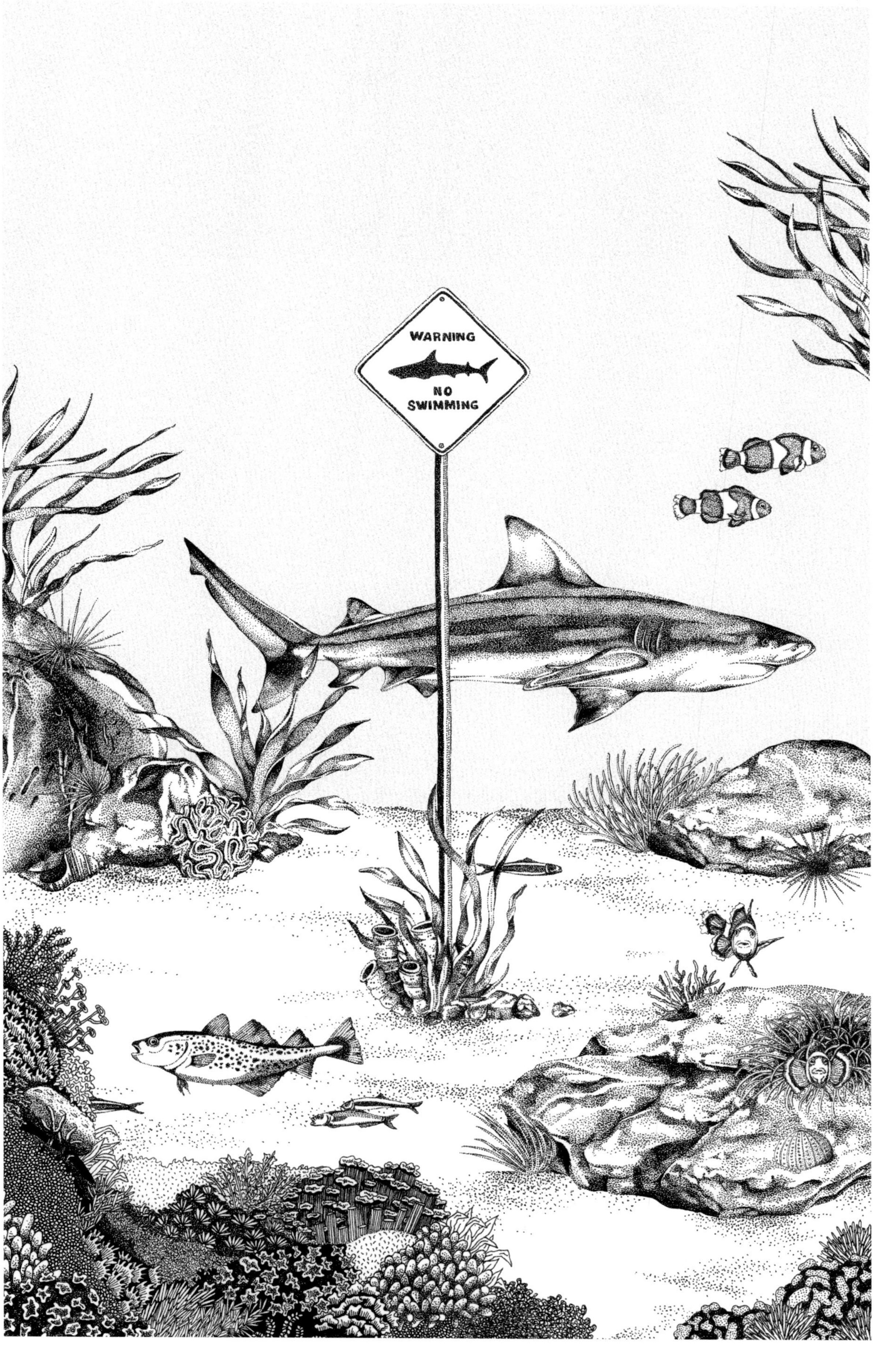
WARNING
NO
SWIMMING

CHAPTER
07

IF SHARKS COULD SPEAK

Deep Blue is the world's most famous—and arguably the largest—female great white. She has many enthusiastic fans and could be considered our planet's official shark ambassador. Whenever she is spotted, everyone is thrilled, not only the researchers and scientists. Deep Blue is a unique great white shark, more than six metres long, weighing at least two tonnes, and she is thought to be over fifty years old. She is also definitely the only shark in the world to make headlines every time she is spotted. And here comes the kicker: positive headlines, mind you! She is treated with awe, respect and honest interest, which is completely different from how we usually treat sharks. I can only hope that Deep Blue stays alive for a long time; she can theoretically live to be around seventy years old—and, of course, she can still keep growing all that time. Since she is not tagged, she cannot be tracked.

DEEPBLUE   904 posts   14k followers   17 following

"What we know is a drop; what we don't know is an ocean."
—Isaac Newton

You're lucky to have met me, because I know my way around the ocean. Much better than that Mr Newton (who never actually said the above quote anyway)! I'm sure he could tell me a thing or two about life on land, though. Now, that is a real mystery to us sharks.

DEEPBLUE

899 posts   **14k** followers   **17** following

Liked by **diving_freak** and **14,467 others**

DeepBlue Good morning, everyone! Did you get a good night's sleep? A funny thing happened to me today—I found an underwater camera at the bottom of the sea. Some diver must have lost it. By the way, operating a camera with your fins and teeth is not easy. You have to place it gently in your mouth or on your snout (timer function). *Click, click!* I know they're not the best pictures in the world, but practice makes perfect. And then later I swam through one of the kelp forests and actually took a good picture! See the diver? He didn't see me. By the way, kelp forests urgently need to be protected, they are super important for us marine animals. Just like these seagrass meadows. Even though I'm the largest great white shark in the world, I can swim right through them without being noticed. I've still got it! Want to see more of me? Well, come on then!

See all 5,000 comments

diving_freak 1 day
I'd also like to go swimming with you!

DeepBlue @diving_freak available for ocean adventures :)

seahawk 2 weeks
where is this kelp forest? I'd like to take a look!

DeepBlue @seahawk that was off California. Shall I send you the coordinates on your mobile?

| DEEPBLUE | **900** posts | **14k** followers | **17** following |

Liked by **VeronikaBlue** and **12,596 others**

DeepBlue Recently, in Hawaii, selfie with a diver ;) I don't actually go there very often. The island is a bit off my usual routes. But the smell of a whale carcass led me there! Hey, don't get weirded out; for me, it's a mountain of delicious food (you'd probably call it a buffet?). And on top of that, I got to hang out with some nice people! And don't think I'm a glutton. Sure, I'm pretty big and need to eat every now and then, but what about you? I think the diver and I could be besties. She'd just have to come live in the ocean! Would you be cool enough to dive with me? Don't worry, I don't bite!

See all 2,999 comments

Honolulu_partytoad 3 days
There's finally something happening in Hawaii, and I'm missing it? Shame on me! :(

DeepBlue @Honolulu_partytoad I'll be back; hold some whale meat for me!

daysofthetitanic 4 weeks
DeepBlueShark for president!

DeepBlue @daysofthetitanic vote for me ;) I can eat that Trump for breakfast and still have room for dessert!

| | DEEPBLUE | **901** posts | **14k** followers | **17** following |

Liked by **Cheshire_Cat** and **256,499 others**

DeepBlue So, here I am, on the run. Really, it even happens in the ocean! Annoying paparazzi everywhere (note: this word was originally the name of an annoying press photographer in a movie. Now we use it for all ruthless photographers)! They just wouldn't stop taking pictures of me. *Click. Click. Click.* And they followed me everywhere. I mean, I couldn't even go wee or anything. That's really not on, is it?

See all 1,233 comments

blackeagle 4 weeks
Humans can be so annoying! I'm ashamed for them all.

DeepBlue @blackeagle Animals, too, I'm telling you. The other day a dolphin followed me, I think he wanted to marry me! Don't ask.

| DEEPBLUE | **902** posts | **14k** followers | **17** following |

Liked by **Alice_in_Wonderland** and **1,455,444 others**

DeepBlue I recently ran into this guy. Orcas really can't be trusted. They even hunt sharks, so you have to be on your guard. Of course, a big shark like me wouldn't be scared of one little orca, but wherever one killer whale appears, others are always nearby. They travel in packs. And they whistle at each other, brrr! So it's better to get out of there quickly!

See all 978 comments

Whale101 1 day
Orcas are weird!

DeepBlue @Whale101 That's what I'm saying!

Greenpeace 2 days
Save the whales!

DeepBlue @Greenpeace Hey, and who's going to save me from them?

Diving_Bell1 4 weeks
I would have loved to have been there—a meeting of the giants!

DeepBlue @Diving_Bell1 I was definitely bigger than that whale clown, believe me! :)

DEEPBLUE

903 posts　　**14k** followers　　**17** following

Liked by **Jumbo** and **21,455,444 others**

DeepBlue And yet another friendly diver right next to me—that was just one of the nice encounters. There really are people who know how to behave in the ocean, who are quiet and calm, completely unhurried, not kicking or stamping or flailing or screaming or anything like that. Why can't everyone be relaxed in the water? It helps us sharks to chill out too, honestly!

See all 978 comments

friendlywoman 1 day
This woman is living my dream!

DeepBlue @friendlywoman make your dreams come true!

Lanzelot54 3 days
It's a good thing you weren't hungry…

DeepBlue @Lanzelot54 oh come on, give me a break, sharks don't eat people!

| DEEPBLUE | **904** posts | **14k** followers | **17** following |

Liked by **VeronikaBlue** and **224,578,444 others**

DeepBlue Here I am briefly letting another shark use my camera—his name is Sammy! He's a blacktip shark. Of course, he's much smaller than me, but we still like each other. I even painted the tip of my dorsal fin black for him (just saying, squid ink!). We actually wanted to take a selfie together, but we couldn't manage it. You can also find Sammy on the cover of this book—he's the one big blacktip shark in the middle. See you soon, your DeepBlue!

See all 9,978,666 comments

totalsecret 1 day
Wow wow! You're pretty!

DeepBlue @totalsecret I'm smart too :)

Tokyoflitzer 2 days
Please write your own book DeepBlue…

DeepBlue @TokyoZoom Maybe I will do that one day!

CrazyGlowworm 9 weeks
DeepBlue, wow, is much smarter than a cow!

DeepBlue @CrazyGlowworm Really? You call that a rhyme?

SEE YOU SOON, MY FRIENDS!

Wasn't our journey into the world of sharks exciting? Of course, there is so much more to learn about these incredible creatures, but now it's up to you to find out on your own!

In the meantime, I'm thinking about which animal species we could explore next. Seahorses? Whales? Turtles? Feel free to send more suggestions to the publisher. (You can email books@pushkinpress.com.) And maybe you'd also like to send them some of your best shark illustrations? If you do, I'll post them on Instagram!

Answers to p. 19 *(Sayings)*:

1. This is justice, Bible style: demanding punishment that is equal to the crime. Shakespeare would have said: to demand your pound of flesh. Ew!
2. Getting very old. People used to think you could tell the age of a horse by the length of its teeth.
3. Only just—so, you might narrowly escape a disaster "by the skin of your teeth".
4. A painfully boring experience. I bet getting some of you to do your homework can be like that.
5. Deliberate, unrepentant lying.
6. To fight really hard, like when you're down to scratching and biting.
7. And don't we all?

Answers to p. 63 *(Shark Quiz)*:

1. Carpet shark
2. Lemon shark
3. Bamboo shark
4. False cat shark
5. Bignose shark
6. Galapagos shark
7. Japanese saw shark
8. Crocodile shark
9. Prickly dogfish
10. Pacific sleeper shark
11. Pyjama shark

Can you find all seven cartilaginous fish hiding here? image: p. 12

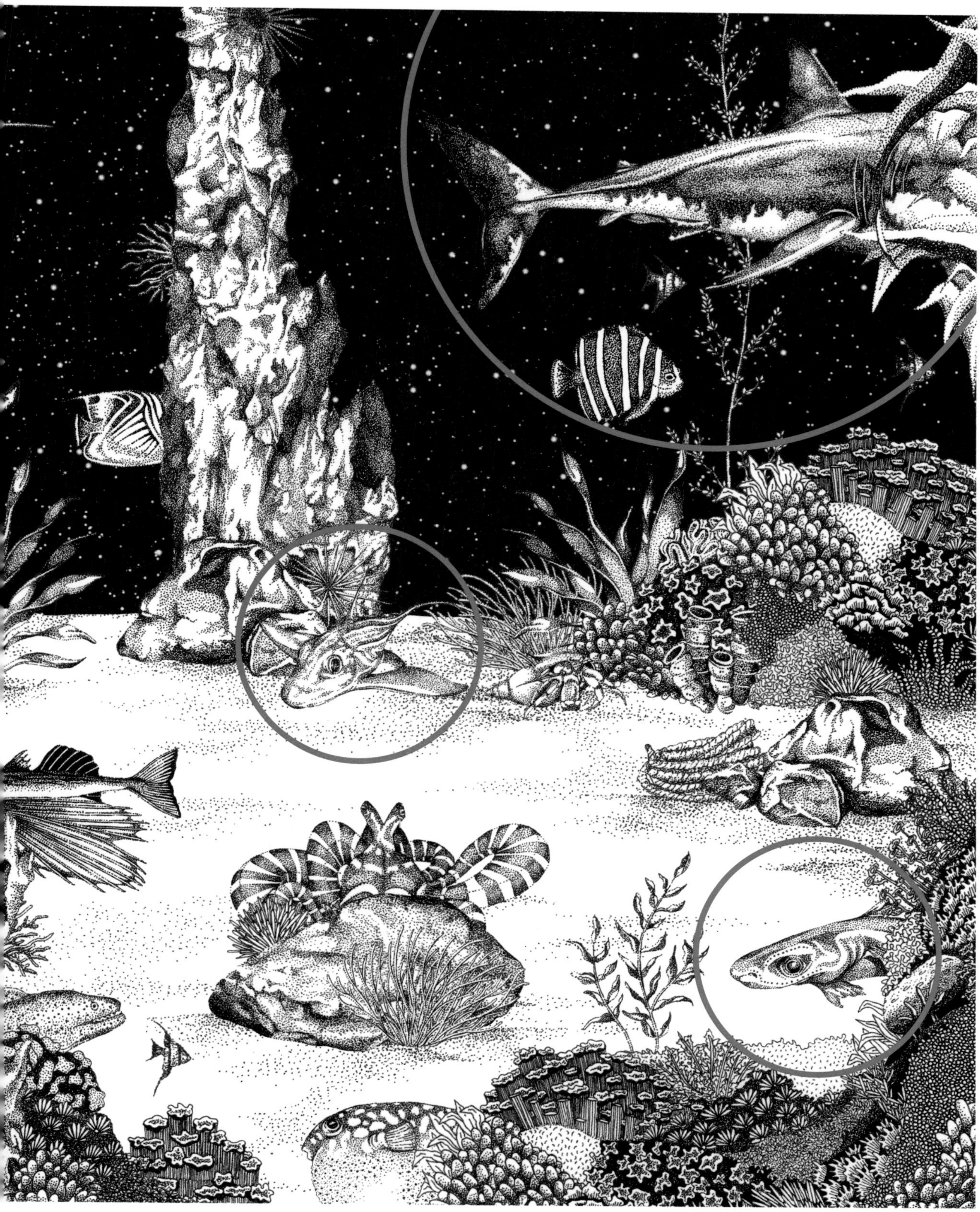

136 ANSWERS

Can you find all of the seven species sharks like to prey on? image: p. 22

AMAZING SHARK 137

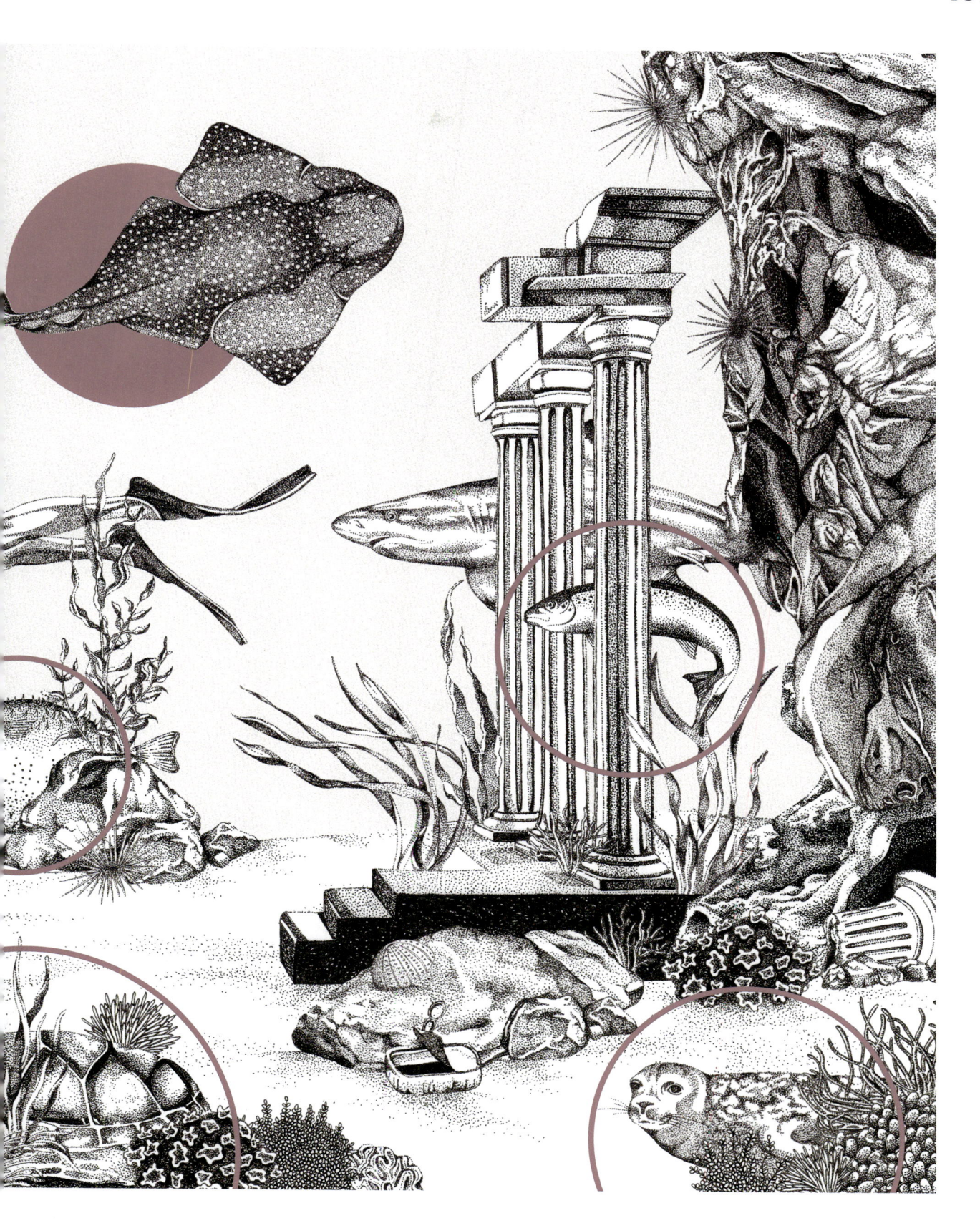

138　　　　　　　　　　　　　ANSWERS

Can you find all seven shark eggs hidden in this picture? image: p. 96

AMAZING SHARK

139

DO YOU WANT TO KNOW MORE?

We have put together a few things for you here—so you can delve deeper with your own research. Of course, this is just a tiny selection. You will discover a lot more about sharks in numerous books, films and on the internet. Many thanks to the researchers, scientists, journalists and others who share their knowledge with us.

FILMS

✦ *Ama*—a short film by Julie Gautier
https://www.youtube.com/watch?v=bdBuDg7mrT8

LINKS

✦ **The Red List**
https://www.iucnredlist.org

✦ **Shark Trust**
https://www.sharktrust.org/

✦ **Shark Conservation Foundation**
https://hai.swiss/en

✦ **Ocearch** *(real-time search for marine animals by name)*
https://www.ocearch.org

✦ **Chris Fallows** *(jumping sharks)*
https://www.chrisfallows.com

✦ **Dive into the depths**
https://neal.fun/deep-sea/

BOOKS

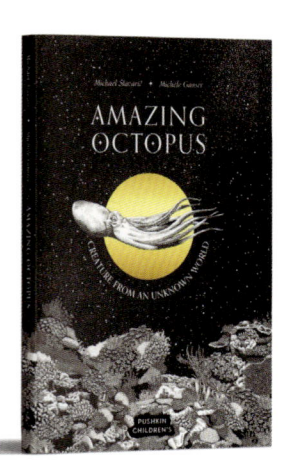

✦ Michael Stavarič & Michèle Ganser
Amazing Octopus: Creature from an Unknown World

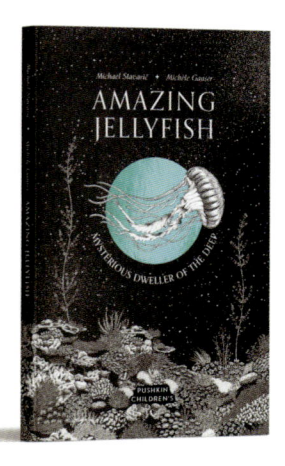

✦ Michael Stavarič & Michèle Ganser
Amazing Jellyfish: Mysterious Dweller of the Deep

Michael Stavarič, born in 1972 in Brno, is a writer, translator and lecturer who lives in Vienna. He would have liked to become a marine biologist. Now he writes children's books, novels, plays and poems, but is still interested in fauna and flora, especially marine animals.

Copyright © Minitta Kandlbauer

Michèle Ganser, born in Aachen in 1995, studied communication design in Aachen and Mainz. She is particularly fascinated by the universe, the stars and the different planets. In her illustrations she combines exciting themes in an unusual way and thus creates completely new worlds. In her free time she likes to read—preferably science-fiction novels.

Copyright © Michèle Ganser

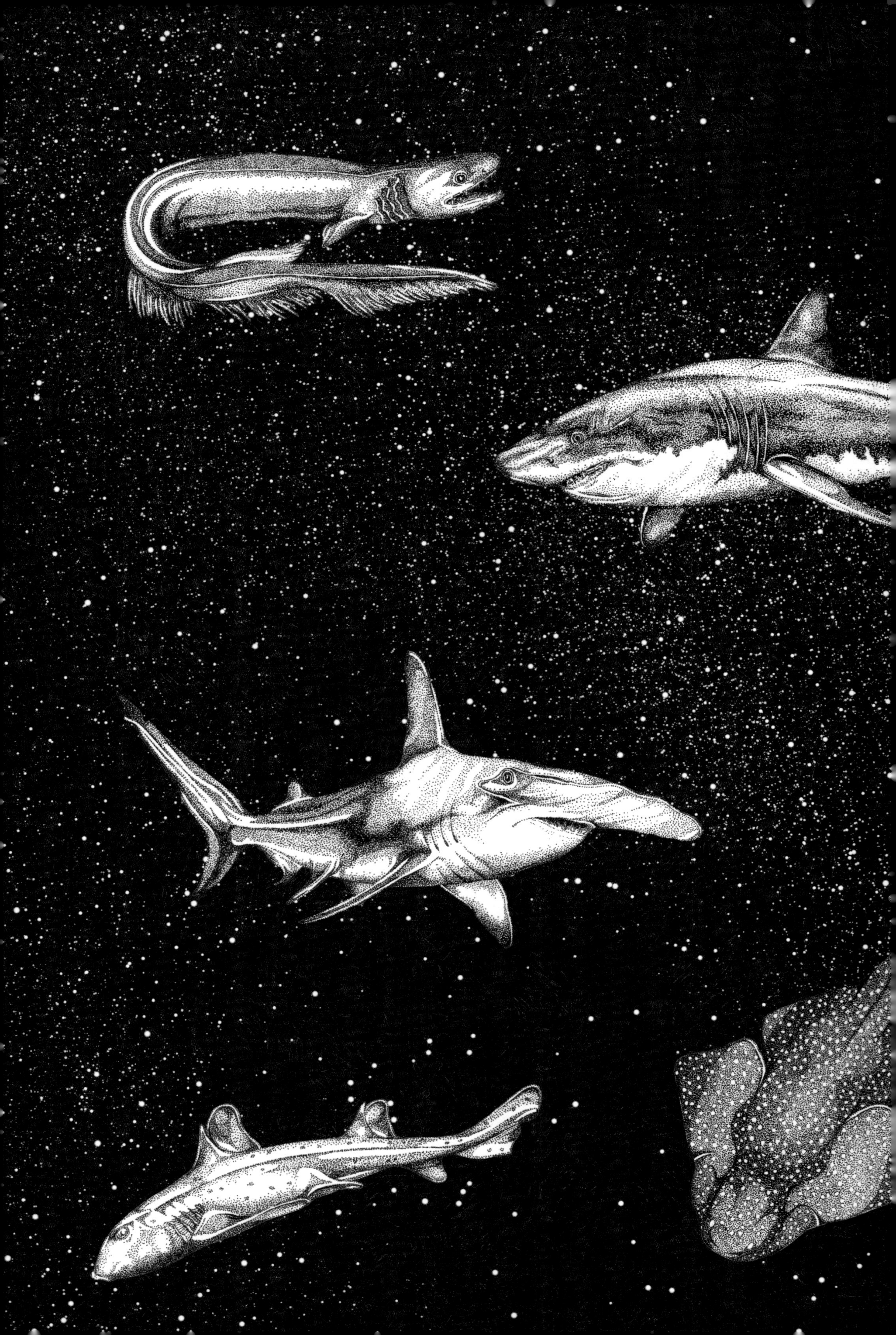

Pushkin Press
Somerset House, Strand
London WC2R 1LA

Original title: *Faszination Haie* by Michael Stavarič and Michèle Ganserer
Copyright © Leykam Buchverlagsgesellschaft m.b.H & Co.KG, Graz – Wien – Berlin 2024
English translation © Oliver Latsch 2025

First published by Pushkin Press in 2025

ISBN 13: 978-1-78269-553-0

Federal Ministry
Republic of Austria
Arts, Culture,
Civil Service and Sport

All rights reserved. No part of this publication may be reproduced, stored in a retrieval system or transmitted in any form or by any means, electronic, mechanical, photocopying, recording or otherwise, or for the purpose of training artificial intelligence technologies or systems without prior permission in writing from Pushkin Press

A CIP catalogue record for this title is available from the British Library

The authorised representative in the EEA is eucomply OÜ, Pärnu mnt. 139b-14, 11317, Tallinn, Estonia, hello@eucompliancepartner.com, +33757690241

Typeset by Tetragon, London
Printed and bound in China by C&C Offset Printing Co. Ltd.

Pushkin Press is committed to a sustainable future for our business, our readers and our planet. This book is made from paper from forests that support responsible forestry.

MIX
Paper | Supporting responsible forestry
FSC® C008047

www.pushkinpress.com

9 8 7 6 5 4 3 2 1